GOSPEL  PSALMS

GOSPEL FOR MUSLIMS

Learning to read the Bible through eastern eyes

Steve Bell

Foreword by George Verwer

Authentic

18 17 16 15 14 13 12   7 6 5 4 3 2 1

First published 2012 by Authentic Media Limited
52 Presley Way, Crownhill, Milton Keynes, MK8 0ES
www.authenticmedia.co.uk

British Library Cataloguing in Publication Data
A catalogue record for this book is available from the British Library
ISBN 978-1-85078-880-5

Unless otherwise stated, Scripture quotations are taken from THE HOLY
BIBLE, TODAY'S NEW INTERNATIONAL VERSION © 2005 by
International Bible Society. Used by permission of Hodder & Stoughton
Publishers, a division of Hodder Headline Ltd. All rights reserved. 'TNIV' is a
registered trademark of Biblica.
REVISED STANDARD VERSION OF THE BIBLE, copyright © 1952 [2nd
edition, 1971] by the Division of Christian Education of the National Council
of the Churches of Christ in the United States of America.
Used by permission. All rights reserved.
THE HOLY BIBLE, NEW INTERNATIONAL VERSION. Copyright ©1973,
1978, 1984 by Biblica. Used by permission of Hodder & Stoughton
Publishers, a member of the Hachette Livre UK Group. All rights reserved.
'NIV' is a registered trademark of Biblica UK, trademark number 1448790.
THE AUTHORISED VERSION OF THE BIBLE
Unless otherwise stated, Qur'anic quotations are taken from THE HOLY
QUR'AN – translation and commentary, 1934 by AbdullahYusef Ali, IPCI
Islamic Vision.

Extract from 'Meekness and Majesty' by Graham Kendrick. Adm. by
worshiptogether.com songs excl. UK and Europe, admin by Kingswaysongs,
a division of David C Cook tym@kingsway.co.uk Used by permission

Cover Design by David Smart
Printed and bound by CPI Group (UK) Ltd., Croydon, CR4 0YY

Contents

Section Three: 'Shame', the Megaphone to the Muslim Heart

Signing the invoice,
my inner voice sighs:
Pearl without Price,
owning nothing,
I owe everything to you
the Only One.

Bishop Graham Kings[1]

---

[1] Bishop Graham Kings, from the poem 'Gallery into Oratory' in *Signs & Seasons* (Norwich: Canterbury Press, 2008), p. 64. Used with permission.

Foreword

You have a very important book in your hands right now, and I hope you will read it. It may not be a book you will fully understand, nor is it one that you have to agree with on every point, but I believe it is a vital read in the light of so much that is being written and said about Muslims.

I myself have been committed to Muslims, and have spoken about them in thousands of meetings. Upon arriving in Bombay (now Mumbai) in 1964, our first campaign was among the Muslims of that city. In the next forty-five years, our organization, Operation Mobilization, was destined to give tens of millions of them the word of God across all of India. The response to all that has been very small, but if I had read a book like this in those early days, who knows how much more effective the work would have been.

It is so easy to have our thinking affected by our own culture; and how slow we are to change. In our work with hundreds of people working among these special friends, we are still learning. Many of us will read this book and be helped along the way. Not everyone knows it, but there is a huge global movement to demonstrate the love of Jesus to all people in ways that they can grasp and understand. Some good results are coming from this.

Yes, this will be a controversial book for some, because there are divergent views on some aspects of the material but, as Charles Swindoll says in his great book *The Grace Awakening*,[1] we need to learn how to graciously disagree and press on. The day of 'straight drinks' in the body of Christ is probably coming to an end; it will be a cocktail of approaches that is needed in future if we are to reach the masses of Muslim people. This will be very messy, but so often God works in very complex and messy situations.

What Steve says about shame is very important and needs to be incorporated into our thinking and action. He also keeps a balance between grace and truth.

We seem to have so many harsh books about Muslims and Islam and there appears to be an increase in generalizations about them. Some reports imply that Muslims are going to take over Europe and especially the UK; for me, these fears are unfounded. I am not saying there is not a large problem – but a takeover is not it.

Here is a book about Muslims that if a Muslim reads it, they may want to talk to those of us who love Jesus to find out what it is all about. I can only thank God as I read this book because its message is urgently needed. More than ever we need to understand Islam and Muslims, and this book will be an enormous help. It has the kind of common sense and balance that books about Islam often fall short of.

Take the step – get involved – read it!

George Verwer, *Operation Mobilization*

Notes

[1] Swindoll, Charles R., *The Grace Awakening* (Dallas: Word Publishing, 1990)

Acknowledgements

Thanks to Irfan for giving me the original seed of an idea in an animated meeting in my office. The seed germinated and blossomed into this book.

In writing it, I am indebted to Revd Dr Paul Blackham and Revd Tim Green for their invaluable theological comment, and to Dr Colin Edwards for his helpful missiological comment on 'shame-based' societies. Special thanks also to Hugh Bradby and Bruce Warren, for their invaluable and painstaking guidance which has helped safeguard me from being misunderstood. Thanks too go to the ever-faithful readers such as Bob and Pat Tichener, Sharon Abbott; and also to Jenny Wyatt for her thorough and professional edit in preparation for the submission of the manuscript.

Finally, thanks to my long-suffering wife, Julia, who has put up with my anti-social lifestyle throughout the process of this book from gestation, writing and the editorial deliberations to the finished product. She may find it a debatable point as to whether or not her 'reward' is to get her husband back under her feet again.

Some of the names in this book have been changed to protect the individuals involved.

To Alan and Jill Wormald
. . . not without you!

Section One:

The Right of Every Muslim

1.

Jesus, Theirs and Ours

The eternal gospel of a world-inclusive love can never be
treated as a piece of Anglo-Saxon privacy.

Bishop Kenneth Cragg[1]

'Why can't Christians see it?'

'See what?' I asked.

By now my friend was becoming frustrated and animated.

'Even as a Muslim, I could see it; so why can't they?'
His voice rose in volume again.

The scene was my office at Interserve in Milton
Keynes. Outside the room, staff were concerned that an
all-out row was brewing between me and my Middle
Eastern visitor.

'But what do you mean by *it*?' I asked again.

The angst was coming from Irfan, a follower of Jesus
from a Muslim background, whose journey to Christ
had bypassed the usual objections to Christianity that
are often associated with Muslim conversion; including
original sin, the Trinity, the deity of Christ and the crucifixion. Irfan was more able to accept such things because
he had discovered what he referred to as 'the true identity of Jesus'. He had noticed how the Bible talks about

the origin of Jesus as being in eternity rather than Bethlehem; a fact which indicated to him that Jesus was 'more than a prophet'.

This animated conversation became a 'light-bulb moment' for me as I realized that the focal point of the gospel in the West is usually Jesus' death and resurrection and our response to that. However, to communicate the gospel to a Muslim person, the starting point needs to be the person of the Lord Jesus Christ himself, starting with his eternal credentials. I knew this intuitively, but I needed help to articulate it and it was Irfan who pressed the point and asked me to try to persuade British Christians to focus on the person of Jesus before the more obvious Muslim objections to Christianity; this book is the outcome.

When we emerged from the meeting and Irfan had left the building, Interserve staff – concerned by the rumpus – asked what he had been so angry about. I explained that he was not angry at all; he was simply an Arab who was warming to a subject he felt passionately about, namely that western Christians need help to tell the gospel to Muslims.

On reflection I think Irfan asked me because he knew I am not Anglo-Saxon. Like him, I am British but not 'English'. Unlike him, I am British born and bred, which gives me both a 'western' outlook – which I will define in a moment – while enabling me to appreciate the 'eastern' outlook that most Muslims have due to my living and travelling for thirty-six years in various parts of the Muslim world. My own bi-cultural background enables me to stand in-between 'western' Christians and 'eastern' Muslims, from where I try to help each to understand the other.

Having promised Irfan that I would take up this challenge, the first hurdle I faced was how to persuade western Christians to take a step back in order to look at things through a broader lens and realize that there are 'non-western' ways of understanding the Bible that are equally valid. Although this may sound strange to our ears, it is true simply because the Bible is a product of Middle Eastern Semitic culture; as such it is closer to the outlook of most Muslims than it is to that of most western people. We would all agree that the Bible speaks to people in every culture and every age, but as westerners, we also need to learn how to read it through the eyes of our 'eastern' neighbours. To do so, it is important for us to bear three points in mind:

1. The Bible is a *record* of God's mission in the world; it is also a *product* of that divine mission in the world, and a *tool* that is given by God for our use as we participate with him in his mission in the world.
2. Each culture has a particular way of 'reading' the Bible, so there are as many ways of 'reading' the Bible as there are cultures in the world.
3. Westerners can learn to 'read' the Bible through eastern eyes, and use – what is for them – unusual parts of it in order to convey the gospel more appropriately to Muslim people. When they do so, it helps unleash the Bible's innate power to impact the lives of ordinary Muslims.

I use the expression 'reading' the Bible in the same sense that Jesus did, when he asked a Jewish scholar how he 'read' the law of Moses (Luke 10:26).

- I became a follower of Jesus from an African-Caribbean background in 1969, which enabled me to read the Bible in a 'non-western' way and also to allow myself to be enriched by non-western expressions

of Christianity. Although these were often established by western missionaries, they are nonetheless
undergirded by patterns of thought and worship,
which resonate more deeply with me than the pre-
dominantly Anglo-Saxon churches in the UK. So
my pledge to Irfan was that I would try to take you,
the reader, on a journey that might convince you
that:

- non-western 'readings' of the Bible do exist
- they are as valid as the western reading we are more
  familiar with
- an eastern reading of the Bible is essential in order to
  convey the gospel to a Muslim.

Defining 'Western' and 'Eastern'

Throughout the book, I will refer to cultural outlooks
that are 'western' or 'eastern'. This is a tricky distinction
to make because the differences are becoming increasingly blurred. However, it is also a necessary distinction
to make because these expressions, while only a crude
attempt to talk about two broad spectra, are vital for the
reader to make sense of this book.

By 'the West' I mean North America, north-western
Europe, Australia and New Zealand. By 'western' I mean
the broadly post-enlightenment Judeo-Christian assumptions, aspirations, values and needs of both churched and
un-churched people who were born and/or raised in the
West, and whose life aspirations and thinking are shaped
by the past history and present context in the West.

By 'the East' I mean the non-western world, including
the Arab world, South and Central Asia and North
Africa. By 'eastern' I mean the broad assumptions, aspirations, values and needs of people from Muslim

backgrounds who were born and raised in the East or within an eastern community in the West. Their life aspirations and thinking are shaped to varying degrees by the particular Islamic history of their family's country of origin and their present localized sub-culture in the West.

These simplistic definitions are further complicated by the fact that Britain has become a cultural melting-pot where Anglo-Saxons are exposed to a variety of other cultural influences – particularly South Asian – due to a long colonial history. During the British Empire, the Muslim world became part of the British story; a destination for immigration and the importation of aspects of eastern culture. Take for example Hindi-based words such as 'jodhpurs', 'gymkhana', 'bungalow', as well as familiarity with the curry house, yoga and the 'Bollywood' film and fabric genre.

On the other hand, the second, third and fourth generation of British-born Muslims are adopting some of the assumptions and values of the 'West'. Many younger Muslims do not even see themselves as 'eastern' at all. In a recent survey, 80% of young British Muslims said they were proud of British culture, with nearly half approving the rights of gay people.[2] My wife and I have both been schoolteachers in highly multicultural areas, and our experience has taught us that young British Muslims draw on either the 'western' or 'eastern' side of their identity, depending on the circumstance. For example, while religious issues are usually located on their 'eastern' side, opinions about the world around them are often rooted in their 'western' side. This suggests to me that even British-born – and thereby more 'westernized' Muslims – will make better sense of the gospel when it is conveyed to them via an 'eastern telling'.

The Non-western 'Reading' of the Bible

Whether our outlook is 'western' or 'eastern', or a mixture of both, there is a natural correlation between our culture and the way in which we understand the Bible. Take, for example, the story of the Lost Son in Luke 15. As the story unfolds, the father sees his returning son in the distance, has compassion on him, runs to meet him, throws his arms around him, kisses him and puts on a welcome party for him to the annoyance of the elder brother (Luke 15:28).

When westerners read the story without help from eastern commentators – they tend to miss some of the cultural issues that are going on. Kenneth Bailey spent a lifetime studying the Middle Eastern cultures of the Bible.[3] As he interviewed local people, Bailey found that their 'reading' of the story was that the father would not run to greet the returning son merely out of pleasure or forgiveness – only criminals and the insane would run in public. The scenario understood by modern Middle Easterners is that if the father had not got to his son first, the community would have inflicted an 'honour punishment' on the son for bringing shame on the family and community. So by throwing his arms around his son, the father was protecting him.

Examples such as this demonstrate how effectively our culture shapes the way we 'read' the Bible. This in turn affects the way we interpret it; in other words, it is inevitable that we all approach theology through a cultural lens.

But what is theology? Alister McGrath explains that the word 'theology' comes from the Greek word '*theos*' (i.e. God) and '*logos*' (i.e. word, or talk). So theology is simply to talk about God.[4] It is like the foundations of a house where the walls are doctrines (i.e. itemized teaching of the Bible) while the foundations are the theology we build the walls on. All theological thinking about God must therefore be biblical. By that I mean it must be supported by the Old Testament, the teaching of Jesus and the apostles; anything less is merely 'scriptural', but may not be 'biblical'.

The problem is that theology is only a human attempt to organize biblical material and make it more understandable to people in a given society. It is therefore limited by culture-bound thinking; hence our quest to look carefully at how the Bible actually presents the gospel and how to apply this to Muslim people.

In the opening quote of this chapter, Kenneth Cragg warned us about the danger of the 'gospel of a world-inclusive love' becoming reduced to 'a piece of Anglo-Saxon privacy'. In a similar vein, Martin Goldsmith – a British follower of Jesus from a Jewish background – has come to the same conclusion about the relationship between culture, theology and biblical commentary. Goldsmith asks whether it is permissible to see Scripture only through the eyes of one particular culture.

I once heard John Stott say that 'all theology is contextual'. It is often remarked these days that not only all theology, but all biblical commentary is contextual, inseparably related to cultural and ethnic backgrounds. A clear distinction needs to be made between revelation on the one side, and theology or biblical exegesis on the other. While revelation comes from God and is therefore perfectly trustworthy, biblical understanding and theology are our human attempts to determine the meaning of Scripture and to formulate this.

We trust the Holy Spirit inspires us in this work, but nevertheless our humanity corrupts both our theology and our
biblical commentary. Inevitably we see through the glass
darkly of our own theological, philosophical and cultural
backgrounds.[5]

One British Bible scholar startled me when he said that
his particular brand of conservative evangelical theology
was 'the best Protestant theology there is'. Perhaps the
best response to this assumption is to ask, 'Best for
what?' Clearly it would be inadequate in a situation I
came across in Ghana where a spiritual power-encounter
was underway when a pastor's house was attacked by a
hoard of demons which would dance noisily all through
the night, on the tin roof of his house, until they were
exorcised in the name of Jesus. This reality is outside the
experience of the British Bible scholar whose assumption
could be seen to verge on theological arrogance, in the
eyes of people from non-western Christian traditions
who know how to handle the supernatural.

I remember the Indian Christian leader C.B. Samuel
pointing out with a graciously wry smile how western
theologians talk generally about 'theology' while referring to the work of Asian scholars as 'an Asian perspective'.

The foundation of western conservative evangelicalism
is the theology of the Reforming Fathers of 'Protestant-
ism'. While these Europeans were motivated by the
noble aim of remaining true to the Bible, their scholar-
ship was done in a historic context, which influenced
their theology and defined it over and against the
dogma of the Roman Catholic Church; particularly the
system whereby repentance was expressed as the performance of 'penance' and where believers were on a

quest to escape their guilt by gaining 'merit' (i.e. God's grace and favour). This 'merit' was believed to be administered to the believer by a priest as he dispensed the sacraments, particularly the Mass. Reformation theologians discarded this form of 'priest-craft' and replaced it with direct access to divine 'merit' by faith in Christ alone.

Bishop Tom Wright said: 'the greatest honour we can pay the Reformers is not to treat them as infallible.'[6] Pendulums rarely stop at the centre and the overbalance towards Catholic Rome was followed by another swing to Protestant Geneva. During the Reformation some important biblical issues – such as spiritual disciplines – became marginalized, while other issues were retained, such as an individualistic approach whereby spiritual experience became an exclusive personal pilgrimage at the expense of the individual entering the corporate body of Christ. As a result, the basis of Protestant theology tends to lean towards individualism in the quest to escape 'sin', 'guilt' and the wrath of God; which became the preferred starting-point in the West, for the telling of the gospel, rather than being the conclusion of its telling.

This 'sin/guilt' starting-point is underpinned by the 'substitutionary' view of the atonement. This draws on the Old Testament legal metaphor of God as 'judge', his word as 'law', violation of the law leading to 'sin/guilt' and the solution being the ritual 'sacrifice' of an animal in the stead of the offender. It has therefore become assumed in western evangelicalism that 'guilt' is the only portal through which the gospel can be presented, which – as we will see – is not the case.

We would all agree that human guilt before God is a necessary and biblical part of the gospel; however, there is also the eastern counterpart of 'shame'. In the western outlook, 'guilt' is linked to what is known *externally* (i.e. publicly); it is based on right and wrong and is therefore quantifiable; it usually disappears after the punishment has been received; 'conscience' however, is felt *internally* (i.e. privately).

In the eastern outlook, 'shame' is linked to what is known *externally* (i.e. publicly) and is assigned by the community; it is much harder to quantify and it can only disappear when and if the person's honour can be restored; it has the potential to permanently destroy a person's standing in the community. For easterners, 'guilt' is experienced *internally* and is similar to what westerners mean by 'conscience'.

This brief definition will be unpacked more fully in the third section of the book. Suffice it to say that, in reality, both 'guilt' and 'shame' are intertwined themes which are equally biblical and valid, like two sides of the same coin. We will see that the Bible speaks into the cultures of people whose lives are influenced by both outlooks; it neither validates nor judges either system. The unfortunate thing is that the western focus on 'guilt' has developed to the exclusion of the eastern focus on 'shame', which is the 'felt need' of most Muslims who will respond more readily to a solution to 'shame'.

To press the point about the 'sin/guilt' issue a little further, it is interesting to note that the Bible actually talks more about 'shame' than it does about 'guilt'. The word 'shame' – and its associated words in the translation of both the Hebrew and the Greek – is mentioned some 113 times, while the word 'guilt' – and its associated words – is found only around thirty-eight times.[7] So why does western theology emphasize 'guilt' over 'shame'? The simplistic answer is that 'guilt' sits more naturally with the 'Nordic' thought patterns of Europe, which are more influenced by the Greco-Roman tradition of Aristotelian logic, than is the case in the East.

When we understand this, it becomes easier to help British Muslims to access biblical truth from within their own worldview, rather than requiring them to become quasi Anglo-Saxons to do so. Thankfully, Irfan's journey to Christ was not artificially forced in this way. In fact he is fairly typical of many enquiring Muslims, in that his search did not actually begin in the Bible at all but in the pages of the Qur'an, where he was astonished to discover that Jesus was given greater accolades than Muhammad; for instance it refers to him as the 'Word of God' (S.3.39); 'Creator of life' (S.3.49); 'held in honour among those who are nearest to God' (S.3.45) and 'spirit from God' (S.4.171). Irfan realized that he needed the Bible in order to explain such honorific titles. The plot thickened for Irfan when he realized that these accolades were borrowed from the Bible and, what was more, that they were indicators of divinity. This compelled him to research Jesus' activity and teaching in the Bible, where he quickly recognized that Jesus was operating and teaching in a cultural environment that was very similar to his own. Jesus' mode of communication was often via story-telling (i.e. parables), the use of eastern hyperbole and wisdom as distilled in proverbs. Irfan quickly tuned in to the eastern wavelength, where Jesus was communicating in strikingly clear ways that he was divine.

The eastern telling of the gospel is therefore an invitation to Muslim people to change allegiance from performance-based religion whereby they relate to God's laws *without* God (i.e. legalism), to the assurance of a personal faith in Jesus Christ and the indwelling Spirit of God, whereby they relate to God's law *with* God (i.e. grace). The gospel invites them to become an 'eastern follower of Jesus' rather than a 'western Christian' – with all the historic and political baggage attached to that term; it is about a Muslim being given the opportunity of belonging to Christ in ways that are both biblically permissible and culturally appropriate; it is an invitation to retain their God-given eastern cultural identity, wherever it is shown to be appropriate to do so, as I have detailed elsewhere.[8]

I have seen such courtesy impacting Muslims as they see Jesus as the rustic Rabbi of ancient Palestine in his true eastern light, rather than as the blond and blue-eyed character of western stained-glass windows.

So now you know how and why this book came to be written; it is the making good on a pledge to a friend. I realize that I have my work cut out as I attempt to convince you of what many are either too wise or too afraid to say – namely that ours is just one possible way of understanding the Bible.

I also realize that even when a Christian is convinced about the existence of an 'eastern reading' of the Bible, there is a second hurdle: How are Christians to find 'safe-space' in which to talk about these things with a Muslim, without the distractions of the East/West political and cultural tensions of past and present? Is it possible to ditch the centuries-old baggage of human traditions in both institutionalized Christianity and Islam? We simply must because it is only in safe-space that we can examine the person of Jesus on *his* terms.

Real life stories of such safe-space are emerging as Christians and Muslims begin to find one another in pockets of relationship around Britain. But what does 'safe-space' look like? What are the blockages to achieving it? And how can we help create it?

An eastern telling of the gospel – helpful hint No. 1

The story of the Lost Son (Luke 15:11–32) is a helpful way of conveying the gospel to a Muslim. The father ran to embrace the wayward son (v. 20), which is a strange thing to do for an honourable Middle Eastern man (only criminals and the insane would run in public). We have seen that the father was averting an honour punishment by getting to the son first. In the same way, God did an unusual thing by coming to meet us in the person of Jesus Christ, who mystically embraces all penitents in his crucified arms.

The father also kissed his son (v. 20b). This shows that the father was not only taking the boy back under the protection of his household but, by receiving him back, he was also covering the son's shame which he had brought on the family and the community.

Also the father took the shame onto himself, which infuriated the elder brother. This story illustrates the good news that Jesus has covered the shame of us, his wayward children, by taking it onto himself on the cross, before clothing us in his own righteousness.

Notes

[1] Cragg, Kenneth, *The Call of the Minaret* (London: Wm Collins Sons & Co, 1986), p. 167.
[2] Wind-Cowie, Max, on the findings of a YouGov poll conducted for the think-tank Demos on the social attitudes of British Muslims, 27 June 2011.
http://conservativehome.blogs.com/thinktankcentral/2011/06/max-wind-cowie-of-demos-british-muslims-are-being-misrepresented-by a leadership that is more-extreme.html

[3] This background was given by Kenneth Bailey in a lecture at the church of St John the Evangelist, Ma'adi, Egypt in 1987. See also his work on parables: Bailey, Kenneth E., *Jesus through Middle Eastern Eyes: Cultural Studies in the Gospels* (London: SPCK, 2008), p. 279.

[4] McGrath, Alister, *Theology for Amateurs* (London: Hodder & Stoughton, 1999), p. 43.

[5] Goldsmith, Martin, *Matthew and Mission – The Gospel through Jewish Eyes* (Milton Keynes: Paternoster, 2001), p. ix.

[6] Wright, Tom, *Justification: God's Plan and Paul's Vision* (London: SPCK, 2009), p. 6.

[7] Hesselgrave, David J., *Missionary Elenctics and Guilt and Shame*, 1983, in *Missiology – an International Review*, 11 No. 4:461–83; cf. Muller 1996:108–10.

[8] Bell, Steve, *Grace for Muslims: The Journey from Fear to Faith* (Milton Keynes: Authentic Media, 2006), pp. 170–85.

Interlude

British Muslim healed after prayer in Jesus' name

A normal Monday morning suddenly became very special when I received an email from the assistant minister of a local church in Lancashire.

I had been leading a day seminar two days before, on the Saturday, at his local church. The day was aimed at helping local Christians to be more effective in communicating the gospel in a multicultural society. The assistant minister had taken part in the seminar with a special interest, because he and his wife live next door to a Muslim family. His wife had developed a particular friendship with the lady of the house.

The Muslim lady had developed a serious medical condition, which left her in considerable pain. She was awaiting an urgent operation to sort out her condition. As it happened, the minister and his wife had laid hands on the Muslim lady and prayed for her, just prior to the day seminar. The next morning was a Sunday and the Muslim lady went round excitedly to tell the minister's wife that something had happened and she seemed to be completely healed.

The lady went on to say that no one else had been able to help her in the way that Jesus had done. She followed this with a request: 'Please will you help me to follow Jesus?'

Minister, Lancashire, 2009

2.

Jesus in Safe-space

The future is not written; neither is the past.

Antonio Machado

The idea of safe-space came to me as I pondered an amazing incident that took place during the First World War when, on the Christmas Eve of 1914 in the Belgian town of Ypres, German troops started putting Christmas decorations on the trees around their trenches. Then they began to sing Christmas carols such as *'Stille Nacht'* ('Silent Night'). British troops in the opposing trenches responded with some carols in English. Next the two sides started shouting Christmas greetings to each other across the area known as 'No-Man's-Land'. Soon there were calls for a face-to-face meeting, so men left their trenches to meet and shake hands. Small gifts were exchanged and some addresses were swapped as they enjoyed a celebratory Christmas drink together.

This spontaneous and bizarre event became known as 'the night the guns fell silent'. It allowed some breathing space for the dead to be buried behind their own lines, where soldiers from both sides paid respects together for one another's dead. As the impromptu truce took hold, reports spread of joint football matches between opposing troops. This behaviour lasted right through the Christmas of 1914 until New Year's Day of 1915.

The incident embarrassed both the British and German authorities, and men were disciplined for it; something neither side would be comfortable recording accurately. At such times, changes tend to be made in order to make events more palatable for posterity. Inconvenient truth has a way of being 'airbrushed' out or else 'sound-bited' in to history. The point Antonio Machado is making at the beginning of this chapter is that history is only as reliable as those who write it,[1] which is usually those in power and whose ideological agenda is dominant.

This was illustrated in a compelling documentary by veteran Australian journalist John Pilger called *The War You Don't See*.[2] This was an exposé of Anglo-American foreign policy, which appears to include a hidden agenda of self-interest such as controlling oil supplies, retaining political power and maintaining economic conditions that are favourable to them. The programme showed how governments reward journalists who report their 'party-line' while punishing those who do not by sidelining them. A notable example of such independent reporting was that of the internet 'hacktivist' Julian Assange and his WikiLeaks website. Such 'truth-seekers' reveal a very different political and diplomatic reality which can be carefully concealed behind the accepted version of events.

Imagine, for instance, what the history of the Second World War might have looked like if it had been written by the Germans or Japanese. Would the Americans and British have gone on trial for carpet-bombing cities? It is not surprising therefore that so few historians dare to attempt a 'moral analysis' of history; a task recently undertaken by Michael Burleigh.[3] His book makes a refreshing change because – without wishing to sound cynical – it is often necessary to be sceptical about those who fall foul of the temptation to manipulate the evidence in line with their own bias or naivety, to the point where what becomes accepted as an 'official' version of events is not necessarily the reality.

The need for Safe-space

Islam, like Christianity, has a mixed legacy. At times Islam can be its own worst enemy in that it lacks the ability to self-critique and requires loyalty to a medieval system that is fairly resistant to any form of change that is not on its own terms; its texts are ambivalent about issues such as the role of women; the use of violence; its poor human rights record; its narrative of world domination; its discomfort with integration into non-Muslim societies and its condoning of coercion of dissidents.

Such issues are a challenge to Muslims who are required to be loyal in a fragmented system where a growing minority are turning to radicalized interpretations of Islam in order to address their social and political concerns. However, the majority of British Muslims just want a quiet life where they can provide more opportunities for their children than they had.

Likewise such issues challenge Christians who need to distinguish between:

a. 'Islam' as a religious tradition;
b. 'Islamism' as a cluster of political ideologies that are based on narrow and archaic interpretations of the texts of Islam;

c. 'Muslims' as ordinary people who did not ask to be born into a system which demands almost blind allegiance.

A 'wholistic' response to the varied needs of Muslim peoples is called for, which includes:

- relational witness to Jesus at the personal level, through practical service to Muslims, accompanied by the willingness to account for the love behind such acts of service
- a theological engagement at the academic level
- more accurate reporting in the media
- participation in the political process where the positive biblically permissible contributions of Muslims to the life of the nation are encouraged, while the undesirable sinister agenda to 'islamize' Britain is exposed and challenged.

These responses are made harder for Christians because of the cynical climate of a secular society in which the role of 'people of faith', whether Christians or Muslims, are neither recognized, valued nor understood.

The Media Blockage to Safe-space

Some journalists – particularly of the tabloid variety – have a lot to answer for when reporting issues surrounding Islam and its adherents. Their lack of ability to nuance the issues has made it normal to portray Islam as a monolithic metaphor for danger, violence, patriarchal suppression of women, anti-Semitism and bigotry. This is a gross over-simplification of a complex phenomenon.

A Muslim told me the following joke that is evidently going around among Muslims:

> A Muslim man was bitten as he intervened to protect a member of the public from being attacked by a vicious dog. The feel-good story of a public-spirited man was brought to the attention of the press. Although accurately reported to the local newspaper office, it was felt that there must be some mistake; so the editors got to work. The next day when the paper was printed, the headline read: 'Muslim attacks dog!'

We should not be surprised then that Muslims are often reluctant to trust non-Muslims. Take, for example, a headline in the *Daily Mail* on 13 June 2010 which spoke about swimmers being plunged into darkness after the Council covered the windows to protect the modesty of Muslim women. The *Daily Express* headline talked about a swimming pool black-out to appease Muslims, while *The Sun* talked about a pool blacked out for a Muslim swim. I live near the story so I unearthed the truth, which was that the Darlaston Swimming Pool, run by Walsall Council, has 250 frosted panes of glass which let light in while preventing the public from watching people swim. A refurbishment project left fifty of the panes without frosting on them. Three women complained and the remaining frosted panes were put back again. Two of the complaints were from Muslim women and one from a non-Muslim woman. Rather than saying 'members of the public complained', it was 'the Muslims'. It is hard to see where the tabloids got the 'plunged into darkness' and 'blacked out' language from, other than to make a mental link with repression. A library picture of a woman 'blacked-out' by a *burqa* was also used.

A report was launched in November 2010 called *Islamophobia and Anti-Muslim Hate Crime: UK Case Studies 2010*. In his introduction to this report, American academic John Esposito lumped together Christianity with Islamophobia, writing: 'Leaders of right-wing nationalist, anti-immigrant political parties, political and media commentators, and hard-line Christian Zionist religious leaders regularly employ hate speech . . . aimed . . . at Islam and Muslims in general . . . At the heart of the debate has been a tendency to see Islam as a foreign religion, placing it over and against Europe's secularism and the Judeo-Christian tradition.'[4]

This, for Jenny Taylor, media consultant and director of Lapido Media, was unhelpfully glossed by the *Daily Telegraph's* Peter Oborne who referred to the exclusivity of the Judeo-Christian tradition as an unhelpful 'false doctrine', urging that it should be jettisoned. The *Islamophobia* report skewed the true picture of the Judeo-Christian heritage as well as the reality on the ground of encouraging Christian relations with British Muslims. The report rightly highlighted the insidious rise in 'hate crimes' against ordinary Muslims that are going on in Britain. But according to Taylor, the report was overly sanguine about the 'islamo-fascism' of a growing minority of Muslims who are being actively encouraged into the political system, under the government's Prevent strategy. She pointed out the irony of the inclusion in the political system of these 'cuddly newcomers' as if that would prevent the violent few, when absolutely the opposite approach had been practised against white working-class dissenters. Taylor claims that there are other reasons for 'hate crimes' against British Muslims including the simple fact of 'otherness', thirty years of government policy-making that has consistently ignored religion and which allows Muslims to go on living in isolation, the pandering to every demand of vocal Muslims for separate development, and the way government has ignored the bitterness caused to the 'disenfranchised poor whites and even poorer blacks'. Taylor believes this to be a 'truer recording of recent British history' and the cause of the 'tinder box' which the hate-crime report describes and from which the riots in the summer of 2011 sprang. Taylor goes on to comment that:

> Some of the fear of Islam in Britain must be attributed to persecution in the home countries . . . where Muslims have experienced torture, peremptory divorce and ostracism for not producing sons, the prospect of honour-killing and persecution for apostasy. The ignorance about this of even thoughtful men like [Peter] Oborne and [Boris] Johnson, is truly staggering. Yes we must not lump all Muslims together. God forbid. But by what mental sleight of hand can we dissociate altogether the violent ones from the texts and teachings that comprise the religion itself, and that keep so many in thrall to obscurantism and fear?[5]

Peacemakers or Troublemakers?

The trench warfare between Muslims and non-Muslims in Britain is constantly stirred up by sloppy journalism. When it comes to the vexed question of the political nature of Islam and the subversive agenda of some Muslims, we need to scrutinize media reporting more carefully, if we are to be balanced 'peacemakers' who pour oil on troubled waters. If we do not we could unwittingly become 'troublemakers' who pour paraffin on the flames. It is also true to say that we must also remain vigilant about the fact that the political ideology of Islam is driven by core texts, which seem to validate such a questionable agenda. Our response should be to conserve our energy in order to take appropriate Christ like political and even legal action against the right issues, without demonising all Muslims. The national climate will not be helped by ill-informed and/or knowingly mischievous comment.

Some British Christians do little to improve the situation when they pay lip service to the *need* to respond to Muslims in a Christlike way, while using strident language and betraying a negative and un-Christlike attitude. Here is a selection of issues, which Christians must address properly if we are going to foster safe-space with Muslims:

1. **Muslims cannot be stereotyped** so it is unhelpful to lump all Muslims together in one amorphous mass, like an army of soldier ants that is bent on the demise of the West. In reality, Muslims are varied ethnically and culturally; they are also hugely partisan in their allegiance to differing – and even conflicting – expressions of Islam. As one Muslim said to me: 'Show me two Muslims and I will show you three opinions.'

2. **Muslims can be defensive** when they find themselves caught between radical Muslims on one side and an uncomprehending British public on the other. Their instinct in today's negative climate is either to defend themselves or to withdraw into their trench. This polite stand-off with the wider non-Muslim society is hampering constructive interaction. The current trenches, in which many Christians and Muslims are taking shelter, are clogged up with debris which stops us emerging into the safe-space of no-man's-land.

3. **Militant Muslims are a concern** to many Anglo-Saxon Britons who are rightly disturbed by the more sinister strains of Islam, particularly prevalent on some university campuses, which were allowed to take root in Britain prior to 9/11. This vociferous and growing minority of Muslims appear to have a total disregard for western values; they seek to overturn the status quo and do harm to Muslims (as well as to non-Muslims) who disagree with them.

4. **Political or military action is the remit of politicians,** not Christians (Rom. 13:1–7). To entertain the thought that the church should be 'militant on earth' in a political or military sense, confuses military action with Christ's spiritual mandate to reach all peoples with the gospel. Some Christians feel the need to retain – or even defend – what was and to 'Strengthen what remains' (Rev. 3:2). Such Christians become prone to support strident right-wing evangelical organizations, which depict only the darker side of Islam but offer little in terms of how to get the gospel to Muslims.

5. **We must avoid nostalgia** in order to come to terms with the fact that we are in a 'post-Christendom' age. Christendom means the 'dominion of Christ' and reflects the political and ecclesiastical arrangements of various imperial eras. A remnant of this may be the church of state as established under King Henry VIII and Queen Elizabeth I, with its parochial system, which Grace Davie points out 'sustains a space within society in which faith is taken seriously – doing so by means of its connection with the state.'[6]

All this helps give rise to the idea that Britain is a 'Christian country'. It is true that Christianity has been deeply embedded in our history and national psyche because Christianity first came to Britain over a thousand years ago. Among the first believers in

England were Roman soldiers who were garrisoned at Shoreditch in London. St Leonard's Church, Shoreditch, was built next to this Roman site and it appointed its first vicar in 1185. Bishop Michael Nazir-Ali comments:

> The legal tradition, in this country, owes everything to the Christian faith which not only mediated the values of the Bible to society but also Christianized Roman law and the canon law of the Church itself. It is these which have given rise to the notion of equality of all before the law and to the idea of there being one law for all.[7]

Also it is virtually impossible to understand English literature without understanding its relationship to the Bible – particularly the King James Version of 1606 – which has permeated the language.

The downside to this long Christian heritage is that it becomes harder for British Christians to distinguish between what is biblical and what is merely a cultural response to what is biblical. This leads to the perceived need to defend aspects of British culture, and also the tendency to see Christianity as linked to geographical territory.

It is helpful to remember that 'Christendom' was based on Britain's past political and ecclesiastical arrangements. This has been well explained by Jonathan Bartley in his book *Faith and Politics After Christendom*[8] which is a description of the relationship between the church's religious power and the government's political power. Christendom is not a particularly biblical idea and most of us now believe that the kingdom of God can never be identified with any state or political system. Yet the assumption that Christendom needs defending lingers on in the minds of many western Christians. Take for example one such Christian who told me angrily, 'We must know our enemy.' Another leader said from a pulpit: 'The only way to deal with [Muslims] is by war not words.' This line of thinking is dangerous because it is more in keeping with the aspirations of the Crusaders than the mandate of the Prince of Peace who said: 'My kingdom is not of this world. If it were, my servants would fight . . .' (John 18:36). He also urged his followers to be active in the world 'as sheep among wolves' (Matt. 10:16).

Don McCurry describes the behaviour of the Crusaders as a travesty of the faith of Jesus Christ. McCurry sees the birth of Islam as an era in which the behaviour of the Byzantine armies would have given the distinct impression to Muhammad and his forces that the Christian empire was all about faith being 'wedded to the sword'.[9] Whether this was actually the case or not, it seems clear that the 'Christian' armies of the Eastern Roman Empire did not model to the early Muslim cohorts an alternative way of spreading political and spiritual influence.

Of course neither can the opposite (i.e. non-response to Islam) be condoned, as was the case in North Africa where Islam, in its early period of expansion, was allowed to almost obliterate the Christian presence. When assertive Muslims go on the offensive to dominate or harm others, either by stealth or violence, the issue of a 'just war' moves to the centre of the political stage. However, the point here is that, while individual Christians may choose to take up arms, it is grotesque to think of the church agitating for war.

6. **The instinct to protect 'home'** seems to be built into humankind as a species. In his essay entitled *Home*,

Andrew Rumsey draws our attention to the fundamental place that the concept of 'home' has in British society, as something that matters as deeply to Britons as the right to bear arms does to many Americans. 'Home' is a metaphor for security, comfort and permanence, which Rumsey sees as 'an idealized place, a utopia, a heaven'. Take, for example, the multi-million pound TV industry of home-improvement, or the theme of 'home' in the political agenda – i.e. 'the Big Society', asylum seekers, immigration and homelessness itself. Rumsey points out that a 'longing for home' is the definition of 'nostalgia' – perhaps our earthly longing for home is an echo of eternity; an instinct that can only be satisfied when we find our ultimate 'home' in God. As St Augustine prayed: 'Our hearts are restless until they find their rest in Thee' and the psalmist sang: 'Lord, you have been our dwelling place throughout all generations' (Ps. 90:1). The Bible invites us to our true 'home' in God and to join him in a pilgrimage from a garden (i.e. Eden in the book of Genesis) to a city (i.e. New Jerusalem in the book of Revelation). This seems to be the answer for grieving British Christians whose loss of a sense of Christendom and 'home' in Britain is causing them to lose hope.[10]

7. **A high Muslim birth rate** has also led to a suspicion that Muslims are intentionally trying to 'out-birth' Anglo-Saxons as an act of *jihad* (i.e. striving for the domination of Islam); a claim that is refuted by Philip Jenkins in his book *God's Continent* where he shows that it is a normal sociological pattern for the fertility rate of immigrant communities to approximate that of the host community within three to four generations.[11]

8. **The lax immigration policies** over the past few decades are also a concern to many Britons, especially

those who are unaware that Britain has always been multicultural. What has changed over the last sixty years is that many newcomers have been non-Caucasians and therefore what some refer to as 'visible minorities'. As a result of recent immigration trends, Christians face the task of being a witness to Christ across cultural differences. Some call this 'cross-cultural witness', which places a responsibility on mission organizations – that have developed such skills overseas – to transfer their expertise to British local churches. This book is an attempt to discharge some of that responsibility.

Giles Fraser writing in *The Guardian* addressed this concern in his response to a St George's Day newsletter that he received from the British National Party (BNP). It referred to the 'indigenous Christian people of the British Isles' for whom Easter is 'a major part of our native culture'. Fraser comments that even the BNP

> have started using Christianity as a code word for 'not Muslim'. A better St George's Day message would have been to emphasize that George was either Turkish or Palestinian and that, like Christianity itself, [he] was an immigrant to these shores. If a latter day George was ever to find his way to this green and pleasant land, the BNP would be committed to his repatriation. For good or ill, this country bears a saint's name that neither time nor the forces of secular modernity can unfrock.

> What we need is to give St George a new look: the patron saint of inclusion and hospitality and welcome, slaying the dragons of racial hatred and nationalistic chauvinism.[12]

9. **The Islamization of British culture** is seen by many people as a threat. Islamization is seen as a subtle process going on through issues such as 'multiculturalism' – a notion that has been driven by political correctness and the kowtowing to the demands of vocal minorities, causing the unfair marginalization of Anglo-Saxons. Instances of Islamization including the practice of immigration of first cousins for marriage, the introduction of *halal* food in British schools and supermarkets, the right to wear a *burqa* in public places, pressure to include some Islamic holidays as Bank Holidays, the introduction of 'not-for-profit' *sharia'a* banking in certain areas of the country and the agenda to have the family aspects of *shari'a* included within British law.

Some assertive Muslims even express the intention to use democracy to destroy democracy, sidelining the Judeo-Christian heritage and causing the demise of Christianity in Britain so Islam can be imposed as the religion of state.

This concern that Islam is 'taking over' in Britain tends to ignore the fact that the vast majority of ordinary, decent and fair-minded Muslims do not fit this stereotype and simply want to get on quietly with their lives and do the best for their children. A compelling example was the dignified call for restraint made by Tariq Jahan the father of Haroon who was one of three young Asian men, killed while defending property from looters in Birmingham in August 2011. Interestingly, on this occasion most tabloid newspapers referred to them by name and not by the usual generic term 'Muslims'.

10. **Western cultural dominance** drives many Muslims further into their trench because they see the West as 'Christian' in the same way that they see North

Africa as 'Muslim'. Western involvement in the Muslim world such as the Gaza Strip, Iraq and Afghanistan tends to be understood by Muslims as a 'Christian agenda' in the Muslim world. As a result, when a Christian introduces him/herself to a Muslim, the Muslim may be cautious because they assume all Christians endorse the foreign policy of western governments and embrace all western values. This muddle can only be unpicked as a Muslim finds genuine relationship with a Christian, through whom they can learn more about biblical values and how these differ from many of the values of western societies.

11. **Christian hostility against Muslims** is another reason why many Muslims are not keen to talk to Christians – particularly Evangelicals – because of the negative attitudes that have been exhibited against them. This is perhaps more prevalent in the United States, where some Christian leaders are verbally hostile towards Muslims.

While certain aspects of Islamic teaching are indeed questionable, and the political and violent behaviour of some Muslims must be challenged and prosecuted, the vitriol put out by some prominent Christians is unhelpful. Notable incidents of this include Franklin Graham, who referred to Islam as 'evil' on the NBC Nightly News; Benny Hinn, who said: 'We are on God's side . . . It's a war between God and the devil . . . the line between Christians and Muslims is the difference between good and evil'; and Jimmy Swaggart, who referred to Muhammad as a 'sex deviant', a 'pervert' and a 'paedophile'; Jerry Falwell, said that 'a nuclear war will happen with the Muslims but it doesn't matter because we won't be there'[13] – this was said on the basis of the Bible references to a 'rapture' which may exempt Christians from apocalyptic carnage.

More recently, the evangelical pastor Terry Jones of the Dove World Outreach Centre in Gainsville, Florida, called for an international 'Qur'an Burning Day' to mark the anniversary of 9/11.

Although more subtle than the above pronouncements, a similar lobby exists in Europe as evidenced in the behaviour of Anders-Behring Breivik who gunned down 77 young people in Norway to draw attention to the need to protect Europe from 'Muslim invasion'.

12. **Distrust of Muslims** is a real issue for many evangelical Christians and the Islamic doctrine of *taqiyya* or 'dissimulation'. This is a minority *shi'ite* doctrine which allows a Muslim to conceal their identity in times of persecution, by suspending the practice of their Islam when life, property or honour might be in danger. The doctrine is contested by *sunni* Muslims who are concerned about a loss of integrity. The concept has somewhat morphed in the minds of politicians, academics, media and the public – including some Muslims – into the divine right to deceive, as a way of furthering the cause of Islamic world domination.

There are biblical examples of acts of dissimulation, such as in the book of Exodus where the Hebrew midwives misled Pharaoh after the order to kill all baby boys after delivery (Ex. 1:15–21); in the book of Joshua, Rahab hid the Hebrew spies in the wall at Jericho then lied to protect them (Josh. 6:25); also Jacob's sons tricked their opponents in order to take revenge when their sister Dinah had been raped (Gen. 34).

It is a fallacy that all Muslims follow the doctrine of *taqiyya* and that no Muslim can be trusted. The truth is that *sunni* Muslims disagree with *shi'a* Muslims

about *taqiyya* and Muslims argue among themselves
about the validity of an 'honourable lie'. All this
points to the urgent need for safe-space. Christians
are well placed to move beyond this sort of sectarian
rhetoric in order to develop relationship with a
Muslim. That is how to ascertain whether or not 'all
Muslims are liars'. It is little wonder that so many
Muslims see western Evangelicals as part of the problem.

Many of the issues listed above are discussed in greater
depth by qualified experts in their field, in a book I co-
edited with Colin Chapman called *Between Naivety and
Hostility: Christian Responses to Islam in Britain*.[14] I list
them here because, in my travels around the country, I
have found that these are sufficient reason for some
Christians to mentally exclude Muslims from the scope
of the gospel. I am struck by the parallel between the
reaction of many Christians towards Muslims today and
that of the Jews in Jesus' day who reacted to Samaritan
people in a similar way.

Like British Muslims, the Samaritan people were immigrants – forcibly imported, in their case, as an act of social
engineering. The aim was to dilute the Jewish race, which
(it was hoped) would weaken their resolve to resist being
subjugated by Babylon (2 Kgs. 17:24–41). The Jews mis-
trusted the Samaritans because they were an ethnically
and religiously hybrid people, adulterating both the
Jewish race and the religion of Judaism, mixing elements
of Judaism with pagan Babylonian practices. Like the
Samaritan religion, Islam is in some respects a hybrid – in
this case it is mostly of Judaism, but also with elements of
Christianity. British Muslims are aware that they are often
resented and distrusted and they reciprocate with suspicion, which perpetuates the polite stand-off we face today.

Jesus would have known that he was speaking into a similar political and racial tension when he told the parable of the Good Samaritan, which would have been a shocking story for his audience because the moral of the story was that it was the Samaritan – not the Jewish Levite or Pharisee – who 'did justly', 'loved mercy' and 'walked humbly' with God – the core responsibility that lies at the heart of Judaism (Mic. 6:8). This is as big a challenge to us today as it would have been to the Jews who first heard it.

Like the ancient Jews, many British Christians see the need to defend their faith against a perceived 'threat'. I have therefore come to the conclusion that the Christian 'trenches' are largely based on fear and even resentment that Muslims have come to live in the West. Such resentment leads some Christians to a combative stance where they see the need to campaign for the defence of Christianity against the erosion they believe is caused by the Muslim presence. In my travels around the UK, I have often encountered the most strident attitudes in people who were born before 1950. They can remember a 'better' day when the Judeo-Christian heritage was more pronounced in British society. They have watched Britain go down – what is for them – a slippery slope from Judeo-Christian values to a place where Britain is only 'culturally Christian' and dominated by a secularist morality of convenience. Rather than seeing the modern context as a return to a similar pluralist environment as the early church faced, such Christians appear to be grieving for a Britain that no longer exists. As they mourn its passing, they carry an additional uncertainty about whether or not the sovereignty of God is involved in what is going on in British society.

Without anything to base hope on, the grief experienced by such Christians will remain unaddressed.

When people cannot grieve properly, other emotions and negativity retain a greater hold until it is expressed in unhealthy ways, such as supporting strident right-wing Christian voices. Christians who struggle most in this way tend to have a flawed idea of history in which they see the need to restore Christendom and revert to a time when Christianity had a higher profile in society, the church of state was respected, and where Christians were prominent in the corridors of power.

What Safe-space Looks Like

So much for the problem: The solution lies with Christians who, as people of faith, are well placed to lead the way to safe-space. After all, it is Christians rather than Muslims, who have been charged by Jesus with the work of peacemaking (Matt. 5:9). Local churches are also well placed to facilitate social cohesion in a way that government cannot. There are some Christlike initiatives already in existence around the country which offer safe-space, which form oases of hope in a bleak landscape of mistrust.

Examples, at the personal level, include Muslim and Christian mothers relating to one another as they wait outside the school gates for their children; a Muslim couple who made daily visits to their Christian neighbour in hospital; a Christian teacher who found a Muslim gravitating to him as a chosen 'spiritual friend' in a secular environment; and a Muslim who broke down and cried when saying goodbye to his next-door neighbour – a Christian minister who was moving house – saying that he was losing a neighbour who was a person of faith, and did not know if he would ever find another one.

At the group level, a member of Interserve's Urban Vision Team who runs a community project in the North West, told me how 250 Muslim people attended her sixtieth birthday party in a public hall. These Muslim people turned out because they know and love her, as a Christian community worker. Another Urban Vision worker told me of 200 parents from a Muslim community who attended the closing event of a children's Summer Club run by Christians in the south-east. Others report frequent multi-cultural BBQs in the London area. These finished with an epilogue and are regularly attended by around sixty Muslim people; another worker in the East End of London reports a special Easter guest service with dozens of Muslims responding to invitations based on prior relationships; still others speak of small *ad hoc* Bible study and prayer gatherings in homes with Muslim people in the south-east, Yorkshire, Lancashire and London.

At the organizational level, on my travels around Britain I have personally witnessed positive stories such as the following:

- Christians and Muslims are meeting over a cup of tea in the back rooms of British mosques, and in homes. Such meetings are coming about as a result of private interaction and the development of trust between individuals. In these gatherings, people are sharing their concerns about their respective communities, and their mutual concern for society. Sometimes a person from one or the other side leads a brief explanation about a feast day or event in the annual calendar of their community of faith.
- One Saturday morning, after I had addressed a meeting of Christians and Muslims hosted by a mosque in Scotland, two imams wanted to know which local

church I was speaking at the next morning (i.e. Sunday) so they could come. They were visibly disappointed to learn that it was in a church nearly seventy miles away. They asked me to let them know next time I was speaking in a church in their town. Sometimes chemistry and levels of trust help create safe-space more quickly than we might think.

- A Muslim leader in Birmingham who relates to a Christian leader in a joint community project asked his Christian friend to go with him to an Islamic school to explain the meaning of Easter.

- A Scripture Union initiative called *Youth Encounters* brings Christian and Muslim young people together to learn about one another through residential weekends and regular local meetings. During these encounters, they are helped to explain to one another the best things about being a Christian or a Muslim. This enables them to reflect on their faith, and prompts some of them to find that they have never really owned their faith and that they are only going through the motions. Through this engagement young people begin not only to appreciate the similarities between their respective faiths, but also to discuss positively the differences between them, opening up to each other with remarkable ease. Above all, they are happy to make new friends and discuss life issues they are concerned about, rather than ones that others (especially adults) think are important.

- In the north of the country two youth leaders – one from a mosque and the other from an evangelical church – developed a high degree of trust and commitment to one another. They have formed a partnership to serve the needs of the socially disadvantaged people in their area. The partnership began when the Muslim youth group did some fundraising for the feast of *Eid* at the end of Ramadan. The money was turned into food for distribution, but the decision was taken to depart from their normal practice of serving only the Muslim community, in favour of serving everyone in the poorer area of the town which included the non-Muslims. The Muslim young people then found that they did not have sufficient contacts in the community to complete the project, so they asked the Christian youth group for help. They have been working together on joint projects ever since, with the blessing of both mosque and evangelical church leaders.

- Christians in Birmingham have told me how Muslims have attended funerals at their church for Christians they have come to respect. Groups of Muslims have even attended church for special events such as Harvest Thanksgiving.
- An initiative called *Impact* has come into being in Britain. It is a network of volunteers from around the country who give joint talks and advice on community relations in schools, colleges, in the community and in religious meetings. *Impact* was founded by Chris Chivers (an Oxford-educated vicar who officiated at the Queen Mother's funeral before being appointed as Canon Chancellor at Blackburn Cathedral) and his colleague, Anjum Anwar (a Pakistani-born Muslim lady who was education officer for the Lancashire Council of Mosques, but became Blackburn Cathedral's Dialogue Officer). For a one-year period, Anjum received abusive phone calls from an Anglo-Saxon male who objected to her working for a Christian institution. He eventually confronted her in the cathedral, but Anjum faced him down, took him for a coffee and explained that the passage in the Qur'an he was citing to show that Muslims were inherently violent should be read

another way. In the end he apologized and said, 'I think I may have been wrong about you.[15]

- An initiative in London is called *Wholly Political*. This is a course run by a Christian-orientated consultancy – Lapido Media – which works with the media to promote religious literacy in world affairs.[16] The launch was attended by leaders from the worlds of corporate finance, business, academics, church and mission. The opening session was at SOAS in London with guest speaker Dr Ghayasuddin Siddiqui, an influential Muslim who journeyed out of radicalism to found the Muslim Institute, which is a centre for the serious study of Islam and the challenges it faces in the modern world. Dr Siddiqui spoke alongside evangelical Christian academics to explore:

a. how both Muslims and Christians have 'sacralized' (i.e. made sacred) their former imperialist narratives and seek to re-constitute them as a response to secularism;
b. how the Qur'an requires Muslims to obey Allah, Muhammad and 'those in authority' (i.e. Caliphs; S.4.59). Muhammad and the Caliphs are now dead, which leaves Muslims divided about what constitutes divinely appointed authority today;
c. how Muslims are divided about interpreting their holy texts for today;
d. what drives 'radicalized Muslims' and Muslims lobbying for a 'reformed Islam' in the twenty-first century.

Such initiatives are creative attempts to open up Muslim and Christian discourse, not only with each other but also with the secular society in which we all live.

- The *Alif* project (name changed) came into being in the UK. It enables Muslims and Christians to leave behind their tribal allegiances and consider the third way of Jesus Christ himself, from an eastern perspective. This ten-week course provides safe-space in which to explore the real Jesus in a relational setting based around a meal. The concept is devised by non-western people and is tailored to the needs of non-western people. Given time, this course looks set to spread worldwide.
- I spoke recently at a gathering that was hosted by the Islamic Society of a British university. The aim was for a Muslim and a Christian speaker to address a set topic from the perspective of their faith group. It was refreshing to discover that not all university Islamic Societies are dominated by belligerent young 'hotheads'. I have also spoken at such gatherings in local mosques where genuine relationships are developing between Christians and Muslims with a two-way agenda, which is a healthy situation among committed people of faith.

Such activities around the country are quietly making history but need wise and accurate reporting in the current climate. At the beginning of this chapter, I quoted Antonio Machado, who is correct when he says that if the true history of the past is not yet written, what chance is there for the present, or the future? So there is a need to publicize such positive stories wisely in order to change the climate of fear. But this must be done well; not merely by those looking for a 'feel-good' story, but by those who know what they are doing otherwise we risk the demise of these 'green shoots' before they have matured enough to cope with the attention. Having said all this, safe-space is indeed among us and Christians and Muslims must occupy it, not least for the sake of the future welfare of Britain.

The Blessings of Safe-space

In safe-space Muslims are freer to hear the good news about Jesus in accessible ways and to be invited to change their allegiance to Jesus without having to call themselves a 'Christian' or adopt Anglo-Saxon ways to do so. It is hard enough for a Muslim to turn to Christ without adding unnecessary hurdles. When Muslims leave Islam the implications are huge because they risk losing their very identity in the eyes of their community who may see them as having become 'coconuts' (i.e. white on the inside); in other words would-be westerners who have betrayed their national, cultural and family heritage. The least we can do is to make sure that the destination of their spiritual journey is Christ rather than 'Christianity'; and that they become 'believers' rather than 'Christians'; a term which was used only three times in the entire New Testament (Acts 11:26, 26:28; 1 Pet. 4:16). The name 'Christian' is not obligatory and is only one of many possible names. In fact it can even be unhelpful and unnecessarily dangerous for new believers. Jesus' call to us is to follow him (John 8:31), to be unashamed of identifying with him (Matt. 10:33), and to take up the way of the cross (Matt. 16:24) – which is not the same thing as referring to ourselves as 'a Christian'.

This frees up new believers from Muslim backgrounds from having to refer to themselves as anything other than Jesus followers.

I hope that one day, new believers from Islam will identify themselves by a generic name that reflects what they have come *to* – and gained – rather than what they have come *from* – and lost. So rather than using the term 'Muslim background believer' or 'Muslim convert', I hope that a more imaginative name will gain acceptance among them, such as the *'mujeddideen'* (the renewed ones), not to be confused with *mujahideen* (violent Islamists).[17] This expresses well the fact that Jesus came to bring an internal revolution of the heart. This is the language used by the Christian apologist C.S. Lewis who described the process of God at work in people. Applying Lewis' perception – which seems aligned to that of the Kingdom of God – the world does not consist of people who are 100 per cent Christ-followers or Muslims; people are slowly ceasing to be one thing in order to become another. People are ceasing to be 'Christian' while still calling themselves by that name, while others (such as Muslims) are slowly becoming Christ-followers, while not realizing it; and certainly not identifying themselves as such.[18]

In this chapter we have seen that Christians need to consciously leave their ideological trench and clear away the rubble of bad history in order to pursue safe-space in which to relate to Muslims as people. When we are ready to convey the gospel to Muslims in ways that are more meaningful to them, we are ready to think about the need for a bespoke telling of the gospel.

The gospel was never intended to be a 'one-size-fits-all' message that can be conveyed to all cultures in a mono-cultural way. But to understand why not, we need to identify what the irreducible elements of 'the gospel' are and what precisely 'culture' is. And how does our birth culture affect the way we need to hear the gospel?

Notes

1. Machado, Antonio, in Louis Werner & Jesus Conde Alaya, *The Past is Not Yet Written*, Saudi Aramco World (Texas: May/June 2009), pp. 19, 21.

2. Pilger, John, documentary programme *The War You Don't See* (ITV1, Tuesday 14 December, 2010). This programme also featured the work of Mark Curtis, the author of *Secret Affairs: Britain's Collusion with Radical Islam* (London: Serpent's Tail, 2010) and *The Great Deception: Anglo-American Power and World Order* (London: Pluto Press, 1998); both books expose the behind-the-scenes manipulation of the media.

3. Burleigh, M., *Moral Combat: A History of World War II* (London: Harper Press, 2010).

4. Dr Taylor's comments arise out of reportage on the work of Lambert, R and Githens-Mazer, J., 2010, *Islamophobia and Anti-Muslim Hate Crime: UK Case Studies 2010* (Exeter: European Muslim Research Centre and the University of Exeter), p. 27.

5. Taylor, Jenny, *The False Consciousness of Western Civilisation* (Tuesday 30 November, 2010), Lapido Media, www.lapido-media.com.
   See also the source article – http://www.spectator.co.uk/melaniephillips/6505289/the-false-consciousness-of-western-civilisation.thtml

6. Grace Davie quoted in Wells, Samuel & Coakley, Sarah, *Praying for England: Priestly Presence in Contemporary Culture* (London: Continuum, 2008), chapters 1 & 4.

7. Nazir-Ali, Michael, in his foreword to *Beyond Naivety and Hostility: Christian Responses to Islam in Britain*, eds. Bell, Steve & Chapman, Colin, (Milton Keynes: Authentic Media, 2011).

8. Bartley, Jonathan, *Faith and Politics after Christendom – The Church as a Movement for Anarchy* (Carlisle: Paternoster, 2006), pp. 34–6.

9 McCurry, Don, *Healing the Broken Family of Abraham – New Life for Muslims* (Colorado Springs: Ministry to Muslims, 2001) extracted in *Mission Frontiers* (December 2001), pp. 24–7.

10 Rumsey, Andrew, an unpublished essay *Home*; see also his essay *Is England Still a Christian Nation? A Sociological Exploration of the Anglican Parish*; and also his talk, *The Last Bus Home* (Greenbelt, 2010).

11 Jenkins, Philip, *God's Continent: Christianity, Islam and Europe's Religious Crisis* (Oxford: Oxford University Press, 2007).

12 Fraser, Giles, 'St George the immigrant', in *The Guardian*, Thursday 23 April, 2009 © Guardian News & Media Ltd.

13 Halsell, Grace, *Prophecy & Politics – Militant Evangelists on the Road to Nuclear War* (Westport, CT: Lawrence Hill & Co, 1986); quoted by Musk, Bill, *The Future of Islam in Eschatology – Theirs and Ours*, Spring Harvest, 2008, ICC Media Group, Essential Christian.com, Eastbourne.
See also: Ontario Consultants on Religious Tolerance, *Attacks on Muslims by Conservative Protestants*, http://www.religioustolerance.org/reac_ter18b.htm.

14 Eds. Bell, Steve & Chapman, Colin, *Beyond Naivety and Hostility: Christian Responses to Islam in Britain* (Milton Keynes: Authentic Media, 2011).

15 Ryan, Nick, *Dog Collars and Hijabs* (Reader's Digest, December 2010), pp. 156–61.

16 Lapido Media – *Religious Literacy in Secular Society*, www.lapidomedia.com/whollypolitical

17 Muller, Roland, *Tools for Muslim Evangelism* (Belleville Ontario: Essence Publishing, 2000), pp. 74–84.

18 Lewis, C.S., *Mere Christianity* (London: Harper Collins, 2001).

Interlude

I found Christ but lost my Muslim family

I am the firstborn son of affluent Pakistani immigrants to England. I had a strict Islamic upbringing in Britain, but I was also spoilt as a young boy. My father sent me to the local mosque at weekends for religious instruction until my early teens. In Islam, a child is born a Muslim if the parents are Muslims. There are two aspects of my parents' faith that I remember. Firstly, a certainty that Islam is the only path to God. Secondly, a respect for Christians because of the sizeable Catholic minority in Pakistan.

I have never lost my respect for many Islamic values and teachings. I also retain much of my parents' Pakistan culture, language and traditions. It is difficult for second- and third-generation immigrants to share all of their parents' beliefs. I spoke English as well as Urdu, watched American films, wore designer labels and listened to western music.

Islam is political. My father always believed that if Palestine displaced Israel, American soldiers left the Middle East and sanctions against Iraq were lifted, then Al-Qaeda would lose support and terrorism would reduce by 90 per cent. We were taught that Jews were our enemy, and that Israel should be destroyed; America and Israel are the two biggest enemies of Islam. But we have to find a way for both Palestine and Israel to exist. No wonder many Christians perceive Islam to be a religion of fanatical extremists who commit acts of terrorism.

The period since 9/11 has been the most traumatic. The focus on Al-Qaeda has finally destroyed what was left of my relationship with my father. The US and the western world must understand the real root of the conflict. They must realize that the creation of Israel is the real focus of the Islamic world's hatred.

I remember the moment when I realized that I was going to become a Christian. It was Easter 1988 and I was 14. I was sitting alone in the lounge of my parents' home in Liverpool, when the film *Jesus of Nazareth*, starring Robert Powell, came on the TV. By the end of the film I was in tears. It changed my life because, for the first time, I doubted Islam. I realized that the Old Testament prophets were Jews, not Muslims, as I had been taught. I now knew that Jesus had died in agony on the cross for us. That night I went to bed terrified. How could I tell anybody how I was feeling? If I rejected Islam I would lose my family, who would be devastated, and I feared they might throw me out.

I tried to ignore it and went back to Islam, praying five times a day and trying my best to be a good Muslim. But I was questioning more and more. Why did I have to bow to Mecca? I knew now that God was everywhere. I wasn't the same person any more. I was troubled inside. I felt that, for me, Islam was living out a set of rules, which prohibited calling God 'Father' or praying to him spontaneously. Islam teaches that if your good deeds outweigh your bad deeds in life you will go to heaven; if not, you will go to hell. But I knew that God was holy and perfect and it is through his grace and forgiveness that we go to heaven.

I had always had Christian friends and I liked the way they talked about their personal relationships with Jesus. They were really nice people who didn't abuse or hate anyone; on the contrary, they loved everyone regardless.

No matter how much I tried to dismiss them I kept getting these thoughts in my head: 'Jesus loves you. God cares about you.' At one point I was so terrified of being found out by my family that I tore my pocket Bible to pieces.

In the end I confessed to my chemistry teacher at school. We talked and he prayed for me there in the classroom, and that was when I was born again. It was a wonderful moment for me, but it has also caused a painful rift with my family, which continues to this day.

My parents were devastated by my conversion when some Muslim pupils at school told my dad, who is a very respected Muslim in the community. At first he was calm, but he confiscated the book of Psalms that was under my bed. After A-levels I studied chemistry at university in Manchester, where I was baptized without my parents knowing. This was a public affirmation of my faith in Jesus Christ.

In the summer holidays of 1995 I had a trivial row with one of my younger brothers who turned against me. He took letters I received from Christian friends offering support and prayers, and he showed them to my father, who made me stand in the middle of the room while he sat reading them. It was terrifying, listening to his vitriol against Christianity as he read my private letters. He was so angry that he visited some of my friends from school to find out how I had got involved with Christianity, which he described as a cult. He locked the door and began to abuse me in the most vicious way, saying that I had brought shame on the family and that he would rather I was dead. My mother cried herself to sleep that night.

My parents thought that I had rejected them, their values, their culture and their religion. Many Pakistani Muslims have little understanding of Christianity, which they believe is a religion for white westerners who have loose morals and get drunk. They struggle to admit their own failings and are quick to pass judgement.

Things improved a little after I graduated and left home to work in the pharmaceuticals industry. My family continue their pretence that I am a Muslim, and my new faith is never spoken about. I do not take my Bible home with me if I visit them. My brother and I are now close. He accepts my Christian faith. However, when I rejected my parents' plans for an arranged marriage, they disowned me.

Ahmer Khokhar, 2003

3.

The 'One-size-fits-all' Gospel

Christians should be like trees rooted in their own culture,
not like TV aerials receiving a foreign message from elsewhere.

Bishop Dehqani-Tafti of Iran
in a sermon in Egypt

A Pakistani lady from a Muslim background had been
converted and baptized in a church in greater London.
On the Sunday morning after her baptism she was leaving the building and the pastor stepped forward to
shake her hand. He asked her in all sincerity: 'Now that
you are a Christian, when are you going to stop wearing
those funny clothes?' Many British Christians still need
help to understand that there is a difference between the
religious beliefs of Islam and the cultural behaviour of
Muslims – including clothing – which existed long
before Islam entered these cultures.

When some Christians find themselves in this situation they adopt coping mechanisms such as the maxim:
'When in Rome, do as the Romans do.' In other words,
if migrants come to 'our country' they should live like
us. It is ironic that from the Raj to the present day, when
Britons are living overseas in someone else's 'Rome',

they seem unable – or unwilling – to adapt themselves to the local culture in the way they expect immigrants in Britain to do.

The 'when in Rome' maxim is just a short step away from also expecting people from other cultures to understand the Bible in the same way we do.

The Resonance of the Gospel

When we take a Muslim's cultural thought-pattern into consideration, we go beyond merely conveying information, to create a resonance in the heart and mind of the hearer. I use the word 'resonance' because I heard a colleague describe the human heart as being like a string on a piano. If the wrong note is struck on a tuning-fork it leaves the piano string dead and unresponsive, but when the right note is struck, the corresponding string resonates in response. This is the effect of the resonance of an eastern telling of the gospel to a Muslim by life and lip. I observed this resonance when an Egyptian friend said to me: 'You are a better Muslim than I have ever been,' and again when another Muslim told me: 'Your book is not like our book. Your book is the only book I've ever read that reads me.' I have described this resonance-factor elsewhere as being like 'a song that the soul once knew, then forgot, but has been reminded of once again.'[1]

Such resonance comes from an eastern person's intuitive sensitivity to the cultural issues that are woven into the text of the Bible, but which often remain unnoticed by westerners. A Muslim friend of mine demonstrated this natural affinity with the culture of the Bible when he and I were discussing the 'wisdom literature'. In Ecclesiastes it says: 'Cast your bread upon the waters,

for you will find it after many days' (Eccl. 11:1, RSV). I
have heard this explained by western Christians as referring to the distribution of the 'bread' of the word of God
through evangelism, and that we can take heart because
results will eventually come from this activity. However,
my Muslim friend's immediate reaction was that this
verse was referring to financial prudence. By developing
the habit of giving (i.e. in several directions), what we
give to others will eventually be returned to us as others
come to our aid when we are in need. He did not know
it but his understanding of the text was directly in line
with the maxim that Jesus taught: 'Give, and it will be
given to you . . .' (Luke 6:38).

Another example is the verse 'A gift opens the way'
(Prov. 18:16). I have heard this explained in the West in
terms of an individual's spiritual gift eventually being
recognized by others, leading to promotion. However,
the easterner sees it as a cultural function that Arabic
speakers refer to as *baq'sheesh* ('what remains'), or a tip
for services rendered – whether before or after the service. This sort of generosity is an accepted social function
that, at best, oils relationships and, at worst, becomes
bribery, which makes Proverbs 18:16 to be best understood as a social reflection on how things get done in
non-western societies.

We would all agree that the Bible describes the people of
all nations as potentially enthusiastic recipients of God's
word. For example they will 'remember and turn to the
LORD' (Ps. 22:27); they will know his ways, experience
his salvation and be 'glad and sing for joy' (Ps. 67:2, 4);
they will one day 'seek the LORD' (Zech. 8:22) and celebrate their inclusion in the people of God (Rev. 5:10–11).
What the Bible does *not* stipulate, is that the nations will
be required to accept God's word in ways that are alien

to them. In his helpful book *Speaking the Truth in Love*, James Brownson agrees – with one proviso – when he says:

> It is all too easy for us to gravitate towards a form of 'spiritual imperialism' that insists on only one possible interpretation of the Bible. On the other hand, we must also be wary of regarding the [Bible] as infinitely elastic and subject to a variety of conflicting interpretations, all of which have an equal claim on legitimacy.[2]

Defining Gospel

But what precisely do we mean by the words 'gospel' and 'culture'? The word 'gospel' is a simplified form of the Old English word 'godspell'. It means 'good story' in the sense of 'good news'. The Old English word was the equivalent of the Latin *evangelium*, which in turn was derived from the Greek *euangelion*. In Greek the prefix *eu-* means 'well' or 'good'. The second part of the word is related to the verb *angello*, 'report' or 'bring a message'.[3] This is why the word 'angel' simply means 'a messenger'. The phrase 'good tidings' is used in the prophecy of Isaiah when he spoke of the liberation of the exiled people of God under the Persian king, Cyrus. This is famously celebrated in Handel's *Messiah* – 'O thou that tellest good tidings to Zion' (Isa. 40:9, AV). Isaiah used the phrase again when he described the messengers who would hurry westward back to Jerusalem in order to tell of the restoration of God's people in Mesopotamia – 'How beautiful on the mountains are the feet of those who bring good news' (Isa. 52:7). Brownson shows how the writers of the Synoptic Gospels describe the gospel as God's coming reign; while in the book of

Acts, the gospel was related to the forgiveness of sins.[4] The apostle Paul used the word 'gospel' to refer to the defining event of Jesus' life, death, resurrection and ascension; and the implications of these for anyone who puts their faith in him (1 Cor. 15:1–5).

Elsewhere, Paul described his calling to take the gospel to the Gentiles, which he contrasted with the apostle Peter's calling to take the gospel to the Jews (Gal. 2:7). This suggests, not just that Peter and Paul focused on different ethnic and cultural groups, but that they both engaged in some sort of contextualizing process in their 'telling' of the gospel. Peter would use the Old Testament in a different way to Paul (Acts 3:11–26; Gal. 2:7–8; 1 Pet. 1:10, 20; 2:4–9).

Defining Culture

The word 'culture' is like the word 'nice'; it is vague and not easy to grasp. When I asked one English minister what he thought culture was, he told me in all seriousness: 'I'm English, I don't have a culture. It's only foreigners who have a culture.' For him, the question was redundant so he did not even try to think it through. How wrong he was. In reality, every individual living in a group is profoundly influenced by the culture of their nation, family, church, mosque, school, club, community or organization.

Simply put, 'culture is the way we do things round here.' Academically put, culture is 'an ordered way in which people do things together' and 'any integrated system of learned behaviour patterns, which are characteristic of the members of a society, which are not the result of biological inheritance.' Culture can also be described as a mental grid through which we perceive reality in our society; it facilitates the human life-cycle from birth to death.[5] Culture arises from the God-given ingenuity of people to adapt to the geographical and climactic conditions around them; it is the glue that holds a society together as people share in the assumptions, concepts and values of the community.[6]

Often it is not until we get to know someone from another culture that we realize how different we are and that the difference is in fact our culture. For those of us who have been fortunate enough to be immersed in another culture for a long period of time, there is the realization that we have been through a process of acculturation; this usually starts with a positive honeymoon period of between three to six months, after which a negative period of conflict sets in for another three to six months. We call this 'culture-shock', after which we achieve equilibrium again; this is a signal that we have begun to bond with the new culture. This process happens because our culture is closer to us than our own skin. Its influence on us is all pervasive and shapes us mentally and emotionally; it even governs our physical movement in public. This is called 'cultural conditioning'. [7]

We absorb our culture by being born and raised in it. Language is the vehicle of culture and the means by which we make sense of the world we inhabit. I first realized this when I learned Arabic and found that language is the aperture through which we view reality; sometimes these ways do not exist in English, and vice versa. So to learn a language is to be clothed in the thought pattern of the culture that the language serves. This is why the gospel must not merely be 'translated' into the words of another language; it must also be 'implanted' into the soil of the other culture, otherwise it becomes a mere foreign import.

Because of their culture, Christians in different parts of the world can reach very different conclusions about certain biblical beliefs and practices. Take, for instance, the anecdotal story of the Dutch Christian who was so shocked that French and Italian Christians drank wine, he choked on his pipe. It is also true to say that the prayers which are prayed by Asian Christians about a responsible arranged marriage for their child, will be different to those prayed by British Christians. The point is that the Great Commission of Christ is to carry 'truth' to the world and not 'culture' – or indeed any particular theology that may be determined more by localized culture than the Bible.

The gospel for Muslims aims at the same thing by making the 'eastern' Jesus accessible to 'eastern' people. James Brownson highlights the need to make sure the gospel is translated, not only into different languages but also applied to different cultural forms. This means we must aim to screen out what is merely a British way of looking at the Bible in order to convey aspects of biblical truth in an irreducible form and without western packaging.[8]

When I lived in the Middle East, I knew Nabil Jabbour, a fine Lebanese Christian who knew how to do this well. He had an excellent way of explaining why a one-size gospel cannot fit everyone, and how Christians must couch the gospel to serve the context of the hearer.

> I wrapped a tangerine with paper. I then taped it and wrote on the paper, 'Change my name from a Muslim name to a Christian name.' Then I wrapped another paper around it and wrote on it, 'Abandon my Muslim family and join Christianity.' Then on another paper I wrote, 'I need to be ready to attack Islam', and I continued with another one

and another one. By the time I finished, the tangerine was almost as big as a volleyball.

Then I went back to the group and showed them the ball of paper, telling them there was something inside that symbolized the gospel . . . I showed them what I had written on the outer sheet of paper and asked, 'Is this the gospel?' They said 'No.' I kept unwrapping the layers one after another until there was only one wrapping sheet left. By then, they could see there was a tangerine inside, and they started laughing. When I got to the last sheet, I asked them, 'Is this the gospel?' and they shouted, 'No!'

Finally, I unwrapped the last sheet, leaving only the tangerine, and asked 'Is this the gospel?' They screamed 'Yes!' I surprised them by saying 'No.' Then I peeled the tangerine, threw the peeling away, and said, 'This is the gospel.' Many times when we present the gospel to Muslims all they see is the wrapping we have put on it. Many times the wrapping is offensive.[9]

Jabbour believes that Muslims tend to hear the gospel through a 'haze of negative influences' which create a kind of static in the atmosphere which interferes with their reception of the truth, to the point where they are not able to hear properly what is actually being said to them. When we start to communicate across cultures, we must stop and think what the receiver might actually be *hearing* from what we are saying and take steps to check what the hearer has *understood* from what they have heard. Not to think in this way does more harm than good. For instance, imagine a Christian telling a Buddhist that by trusting Christ they can be 'born again' (John 3:3). The Buddhist is likely to react negatively because his aim in life is to stop the cycle of re-birth through reincarnation.[10] Similarly, when a Christian tells a Muslim that 'Jesus Christ is the Son of God' they are likely to react negatively to such language of physical procreation. Some Muslim people actually think Christians believe the Trinity consists of God the Father, Mary the mother and Jesus their baby by a physical relationship.

Cross-cultural Communication

Such examples show us that it is unhelpful – and even counter-productive – to convey the gospel to non-westerners in the same way we received it. Senegalese Christian scholar Lamin Sanneh helps us to avoid getting it wrong by identifying two approaches to transmitting the gospel: namely 'translation' or 'diffusion'. The 'diffusion' of the gospel is what I have called the 'one-size-fits-all' approach, where the receiver of the message is required to adopt the language, culture and practices of the messenger. The recipient becomes a proselyte by observing the external behaviour of the messenger. Islam has required this to a large extent; as have some Christians, particularly during the colonial era of mission.

In contrast, the 'translation' of the gospel is a bespoke telling which adapts the message to the cultural milieu of the hearer. This approach follows the apostolic pattern in the early church, which saw other cultures as a neutral and appropriate soil for the gospel to be sown into, take root and blossom locally. 'Translation' enables believers in Jesus to become 'trees rooted in their own culture', a phrase I heard Bishop Dehqani-Tafti of Iran use on one of his visits to Egypt. Lamin Sanneh insists: 'the gospel is bigger than any one cultural expression of it.' He goes on to say:

No one [culture] is the exclusive or normative standard for anyone else and no one culture is God's exclusive favourite. This radical pluralism has theological roots; a situation which institutional Christianity has found difficult to accept or to honour.[11]

Christianity in a Local Context

When I returned to Britain after being expelled from Egypt by the secret police, I had a vivid dream of a culturally appropriate church that was thriving in the UK. It was serving the needs of people from a variety of Muslim backgrounds.[12] Its members saw Islam as their *heritage* (i.e. background) while Jesus Christ had become their *inheritance* (i.e. future). Such worshipping communities are forming around the world. The identity, dress and patterns of worship sometimes appear to be closer to a Christ-centred sect of Islam than they are to a 'Christian church'. Such people-movements to Christ are coming about without outside help; although they are in some sense 'beyond Christianity', they are 'inside the kingdom of God' and 'under the leadership of the King'.[13]

This raises the question of how far is it possible to believe without belonging to institutional Christianity as we know it in the West. Whatever we may think, people from Muslim backgrounds are changing their religious allegiance to Jesus Christ as their Saviour, while still belonging to the culture and community of their birth.[14]

While the voices of eastern believers are important, the possible danger is 'syncretism' (i.e. the merging of biblical truth with other thought patterns and practices). We must be careful to respond appropriately where errors creep in. We must not assume that everything these Christ-followers believe and do is biblically permissible; on the other hand, neither should we be too quick to impose western ways on them – to do so would be to slip into a spiritual form of imperialism. Instead we should be slower to condemn what God appears to be blessing, while addressing the issues it raises. For example the Islamic practice of prayer, giving and fasting are all biblically permissible themes but they must become re-orientated into the way of Christ.

Rather than Christians battling out such issues in an atmosphere of 'theological tribalism', we should learn from the New Testament church and come alongside Christ-followers from Islam in order to 'explain the way of God more adequately' to them (see Acts 18:26).

The early Jewish followers of Christ wrestled with precisely these issues when they debated how God's grace in Christ was to be held in tension with the requirements of the law of Moses and how – if at all – Gentiles could be included in the largely Jewish church. The model which the apostle Paul provided for believers in Jesus from a Jewish background has obvious application for believers from Muslim backgrounds who face similar decisions.

A colleague of mine wrote his doctoral thesis on the beliefs about Jesus in such groups. He interviewed over a thousand followers of Jesus from a Muslim background in a South Asian country. These Christ-followers wear local dress and meet in locations that are simply called 'meeting place' rather than 'church'. These meeting places are decorated in an eastern style with carpeted floors without chairs. Some devise an alternative *kalima* (creed), so instead of saying 'There is no god but God and Muhammad is his messenger' they say things such as 'There is no god but God and Jesus is the Way [i.e. to God].' Some of them continue to use the Muslim positions for prayer, which were arguably borrowed from the Orthodox Church which was using them for centuries before Islam began.

These Christ-honouring groups observe a gender separation in their worship; something Eastern Orthodox Christians have done for centuries. So to help someone of another culture to follow Christ within their own cultural framework is not new; how to do it has been a big question since the early church.

The Rite of Circumcision

An important issue for Jews and Muslims is circumcision. This ritual was first given to Abraham and was practised by Jews (Gen. 17). Circumcision is the surgical removal of the male foreskin and was a covenantal sign of membership in the community of God. It was also a visible reminder to Jews of their religious obligation. The practice of circumcision is a point of connection for Muslims, for whom it is also a sign of belonging in – what is for them – the Abrahamic community of Islam.

The rite of circumcision was transformed by Jesus' death, which replaced external circumcision with the internal circumcision of the human heart by the Spirit of God as he cuts away the fleshly instincts in our fallen human nature. This reality was not grasped immediately by the early church, which was disturbed by groups of Christians who insisted that if Gentiles wanted to join the church they should still submit to circumcision. A special church council met in Jerusalem to consider the matter and decided to resist the move, concluding that the gospel should be available to non-Jews without the requirement that they become culturally Jewish in order to do so: 'we should not make it difficult for the Gentiles who are turning to God . . . [Let them] abstain from food polluted by idols, from sexual immorality, from the meat of strangled animals and from blood' (Acts 15:19–20).

It comes as good news for Muslims when they hear the apostle Paul affirm that followers of Jesus from all cultures are 'truly circumcised' (see Phil. 3:3 RSV) because they serve God out of a renewed nature (Rom. 2:28–9). Paul also urged both Jewish and Gentile believers to realize that through the cross, their relationship to circumcision was changed as part of a repositioning of humanity in relation to the law of Moses (Rom. 2:17–29). Those who are uncircumcised but keep the law are as acceptable to God as someone who is circumcised (Rom. 2:25–6). Paul also insisted that internal faith in Christ came before external circumcision; just as it did for Abraham whose faith made him righteous in God's sight *before* he was circumcised (Rom. 4:10). Such teaching by the apostle Paul enabled Jewish believers to:

- see the person of Jesus Christ as the fulfilment of the religious system of Judaism
- re-orientate their spiritual allegiance to Jesus while remaining culturally Jewish
- retain their Jewish identity after they were 'defined out' of the Jewish community by ostracism.

The same process should be made available to Muslim-background believers in Jesus who are also likely to be 'defined out' of their community. We must support them in following Jesus in ways that retain as much resonance with their birth culture as is appropriate and biblically permissible.

Temple Worship

The early Jewish followers of Christ experienced an overhaul of their relationship to Judaism, while they maintained cultural and social ties to the Jewish community; this included attending temple prayers (Acts 3:1). So close was the identification with Jewish culture, they were perceived to be a sect of Judaism with Jesus as its Rabbi, which earned them the title 'Nazarene sect', with the apostle Paul as 'ringleader' (Acts 24:5, 14).

As a 'follower of the way', Paul continued as a worshipper at the temple (v. 11). He still believed 'everything that is in accordance with the Law and that is written in the Prophets, and I have the same hope in God as these people themselves have, that there will be a resurrection of both the righteous and the wicked' (vv. 14–15).

Clearly Paul did not replace the law of Moses with the gospel – but neither did he allow the law of Moses to negate the gospel, which is a delicate balance that has been ably dealt with by a Jewish follower of Jesus, Richard Harvey, in his book *Mapping Messianic Theology*.[15] The apostle Paul claimed to have achieved the balance when he declared that he had a 'clear conscience' on the matter before God and people (Acts 24:16); a position that is consistent with Jesus who came not to abolish the law of Moses but to fulfil it (Matt. 5:17).

Paul emphasized his Jewish theological credentials when he needed to (Gal. 1:13–14; Phil. 3:4–7); and as a follower of Jesus from an ultra-Orthodox Jewish background, an equivalent conversion to Paul's today might be a senior *sheikh* from a top-ranking Islamic institution, such as Al-Azhar University Cairo.

Although expert in Moses' law, in the sovereignty of God, Paul's life work was to plant the gospel in the soil of the non-Semitic world. I often wonder what might have happened if he had gone to Arabia, which would have changed the context into which Muhammad was born:

> To the Jews I became like a Jew, to win the Jews. To those under the law I became like one under the law (though I myself am not under the law), so as to win those under the law . . . Do not cause anyone to stumble, whether Jews, Greeks or the church of God – even as I try to please everyone in every way. For I am not seeking my own good but the good of many, so that they may be saved . . . Follow my example as I follow the example of Christ (1 Cor. 9:20, see also vv. 21–23; 10:32–3; 11:1).

Paul urged Jewish followers of Christ not to put any 'stumbling block in anyone's path [i.e. Gentiles], so that our ministry will not be discredited' (2 Cor. 6:3). For Paul, the aim was not merely to *tell* followers of Christ how to live but to *model* how to live. He did this by becoming 'all things to all people' (1 Cor. 9:22b). He also urged that we should not 'cause anyone to stumble, whether Jews [or] Greeks' (1 Cor. 10:32), including not being culturally offensive. Ultimately Paul's motto was that the only offence we cause should be the offence of the cross (Gal. 5:11).

In this chapter we have argued the case that the gospel is not a 'one-size-fits-all' affair and that it is therefore possible – unintentionally – to distort or miscommunicate the message when we convey it to someone from another cultural outlook. So if the gospel is not a 'one-size-fits-all' message, what is 'eastern' about it? Which biblical passages or themes resonate most easily with 'eastern' people? What can we do to help a Muslim connect with the Bible's 'easternness'?

To answer such questions we now embark on a whis-tle-stop tour of the Bible, in which we will see Jesus – particularly through the Old Testament – who is best able to provoke a Muslim to engage with the gospel.

Notes

[1] Bell, Steve D., *Grace for Muslims* (Milton Keynes: Authentic Media, 2006), p. 86.

[2] Brownson, James V., *Speaking the Truth in Love – New Testament Resources for a Missional Hermeneutic* (Harrisburg: Trinity Press International, 1998), p. 34.

[3] Bruce F.F., *First-century Faith – Christian Witness in the New Testament* (Leicester: Inter-Varsity Press), 1959.

[4] Brownson, James V., *Speaking the Truth in Love – New Testament Resources for a Missional Hermeneutic* (Harrisburg: Trinity Press International, 1998), p. 47.

[5] Heibert, Paul G., *Cultural Anthropology* (USA: J.B. Lippincote Co., 1976), p. 25.

[6] Kraft, Charles, *Christianity in Culture* (Mary Knoll: Orbis Books, 1979).

[7] Luzbetak, Louis L., *The Church and Cultures* (Pasadena: William Carey Library, 1976).

[8] Brownson, James V., *Speaking the Truth in Love – New Testament Resources for a Missional Hermeneutic* (Harrisburg: Trinity Press International, 1998), p. 1.

[9] Jabbour, Nabil, *Unshackled and Growing – Muslims and Christians on the Journey to Freedom* (Colorado Springs: Dawson Media, 2006), pp. 22–3.

[10] Burnett, David, *The Spirit of Buddhism* (London: Monarch, 1996).

[11] Sanneh, Lamin, *Translating the Message: the Missionary Impact on Culture, 2nd Edition* (Mary Knoll: Orbis Books, 2009), p. 35.

[12] Bell, Steve D., *Grace for Muslims* (Milton Keynes: Authentic Media, 2006), p. 181.

[13] Higgins, Kevin, *Beyond Christianity: Insider Movements and the Place of the Bible and the Body of Christ in New Movements to Jesus*. A plenary paper presented at Tokyo 2010 Mission Consultation in Mission Frontiers (Pasadena: US Centre for World Mission, July–Aug 2010), p. 12.

[14] Edwards, Colin, *Believing without Belonging (Oslo: Norwegian Journal of Missiology*, Vol. 64, 3–4, 2010), pp. 195–210.

[15] Harvey, Richard, *Mapping Messianic Theology: A Constructive Approach* (studies in Messianic Jewish Theology) (Carlisle: Paternoster Press, 2009).

Interlude

Muslim Man Finds Christ in Hospital

A few years ago at the hospice where I nursed, a Pakistani Muslim man called Fiaz was admitted. He was terminally ill. He came in for short periods over several years for pain control, and later for respite for his wife as he became more ill. Latterly the frequency of his visits increased.

When I first met Fiaz, I noted that he was a really good-looking man with a delightful smile. He was a quiet man, but not at all unsociable. In fact he was much friendlier than I would have expected a Muslim man to be. He had lots of friends and family, and many men came to visit him in their flowing robes; usually in groups. They always spoke Urdu and it was clear that they were much more religious than Fiaz was. They were very sombre, which sent cold shivers running down my spine. They had a presence about them that was not very comfortable for me. Of course Fiaz had his special diet with no pork or pork derivatives, and sometimes the family would bring in a favourite curry for him. Apart from that, he was treated in the same way as other patients, with daily baths and physio sessions and even aromatherapy, which he liked.

When I was on duty I was in a specially privileged position because it enabled me to offer to pray with each patient according to their wishes, and Fiaz always asked for prayer. It was always made clear that I would pray in the name of Jesus. The prayer was less for his healing and more about his day and his family or anything else which was important to him. So after praying with Fiaz I would often talk about the God who loves us and who sent Jesus to be the Saviour of the world. We would discuss such things when I was involved with his personal care, including his bath and hair-wash time, which is when he loved to share stories.

I would tell Fiaz about Jesus' love for him and how he died on our behalf. As a result of several visits to the ward as an in-patient, he wanted to talk about dying; yet he was never morbid. He always listened quietly to what I had to say and read little booklets I left with him. On one occasion when I returned from holiday, I was amazed to see Fiaz still with us, as I had not seen him for some time and there had been a long gap. I wondered whether he had died but when I walked in, there he was, very weak but with the same lovely smile. I quickly learned from the doctor that Fiaz had been asking for me and that they had not expected him to last until I got back.

As soon as I was free I went to see Fiaz. He told me that he had accepted Jesus as his Saviour – he was radiant! Later that morning a morbid mullah and an imam came in with three or four other Muslim men. They stood around the bed with their eyes closed, mumbling away. I was due to go off duty and went to say goodbye to Fiaz from a short distance away from the group. To my surprise – while the visiting delegation were engrossed in their prayers – Fiaz lifted his head from the pillow, looked over and winked at me; then he stuck his thumb up in victory – a gesture that said it all. When I arrived home half an hour later the phone was ringing to say that he had gone to be with the Lord.

It was a Sunday afternoon – what a wonderful day it was for him to go home. Muslim burial happens soon after death and so his wife apologized that he had been buried as a Muslim. She had no time to change that arrangement. Her daughter was later married in a church, because she knew her father would have wanted that.

Nurse, Preston, 2009

Section Two:

Jesus Throughout the Bible

Interlude

Afghans meet Christ in detention centre

We first met 'K' in England three years ago. He is an Afghan man in his early thirties who has a gentle smile but a tired look about him. After a while we lost track of him until a few weeks ago, when he suddenly turned up at our church. He told us his story: both he and his friend 'A' had become frustrated at the lack of progress in their asylum applications, and had fled to Austria. There they were befriended by evangelists who helped them to a personal faith in Jesus. Instead of finding asylum in Austria, they found themselves under even more restrictions. Ignoring the advice of the local pastor, they impetuously returned to England.

Determined to come clean and tell the truth, they explained to the British authorities that they had lied previously and that now – as followers of Jesus – they were telling the truth. There was no getting round the long wait to discover what judgement the Home Office would give on their case. They were immediately put into a local detention centre and told they would probably be sent back to Afghanistan. While in custody, the two friends read the Bible, worshipped in the chapel and shared their new-found faith with their Muslim inmates. This prompted a hostile reaction. Some Afghans said, 'If we are sent back to Afghanistan on the same flight as you, we will kill you before we land at the airport.'

'K' and 'A' quickly learned that this was no idle threat because, during a riot in their wing, thirty angry Afghan young men tried to break into their room to kill 'K'.

Even efforts by their solicitors to get them bail before they were attacked again failed. Then one evening 'K' was told, 'Here are your papers, you are free to go.' 'K' didn't want to leave without his friend 'A' but he had no choice and quickly found himself out on the street with a few belongings in a bag and a bus ticket. As 'K' talked to us, it was clear that his heart was still with his friend 'A', and he asked us if we would get involved.

The next incident was a crucial moment in the story. 'K's' friend 'A' was told one morning to gather his belongings as he was to be deported immediately to Afghanistan. As he boarded the bus, he realized he was going with all the other Afghans who had threatened to kill him. He spent the short journey in desperate prayer that God would spare his life. At the airport they were taken by shuttle-bus which stopped outside the airplane on the tarmac. Each detainee filed out with their prison guard in close attendance. As it happened, 'A' was the last detainee to get off the bus. Then a hand touched his shoulder; it was the last prison guard. 'Your prayers have been answered; we haven't got enough staff to go with you so you have to come back with us.'

'A' was the only detainee out of the whole busload who was returned on that day. A few days later, 'A' was released in the same inexplicable way as 'K' was. When they were reunited they immediately started coming to our church. We now have Bible studies each week. As we read the Bible together, these two men are clearly hungry for God and his word. They digest the Bible passages with an enthusiasm that shows they truly know what grace is and how close they came to losing their lives for Christ.

Urban Vision worker, Essex, 2009

4.

Jesus in the Old Testament

> Jesus was the only person in history ever to come into time
> from a prior existence.
>
> *Harry Blamires*[1]

If the Lord Jesus Christ himself is the gospel for Muslims, the message stands or falls on his identity. Who Jesus *is* validates what he *did* and sets him apart from all other prophets. So when a Muslim person understands the biblical Jesus, their objections to the gospel can be approached differently. This is why I devote this chapter to Jesus' divine credentials.

The Bible is clear that Jesus occupies a unique category that sets him apart from all other human beings that have ever lived – including Muhammad. Many Christians – let alone Muslims – are surprised to discover that Jesus was at work on the earth throughout the Old Testament – i.e. *before* his incarnation. Such material is causing enquiring Muslims, such as my friend Irfan, to conclude that if true, Jesus must be 'much' more than a mere prophet of Islam. The Bible shows that:

- Jesus is the eternal 'Alpha and Omega' or the 'A-Z' of all existence (Rev. 1:8), with no beginning or end (Heb. 7:3)

- Jesus was an agent of the creation
- the Bible includes Jesus in the divine name of *elohim*
- Jesus made a series of pre-incarnational visits to earth before his birth in Bethlehem
- Jesus demonstrated divine authority over every aspect of life – physical and spiritual
- at the cross, Jesus became our Saviour with the ultimate solution to humankind's deepest need.

The claim that Jesus walked the earth in other guises before his incarnation is a huge one – but it is the only reasonable conclusion that can be drawn from the sort of incidents in the Bible that you are about to see. A mystery visitor repeatedly intervened in the Old Testament narrative. He is clearly more than mere man or angel because he is treated as divine by all who meet him.

I invite you to join me and the various scholars who are convinced by the evidence that this unearthly character was Jesus. If he is not, it creates a much bigger problem with no other valid solution to date.

For me, the examination of this claim began as a cerebral exercise; it ended in worship. So I encourage you to approach this section of the book with a worshipping heart, as well as the full critical faculty of your mind. We will use what some theologians call a 'narrative exegesis'. This means we will take into account from the text, the cultural and circumstantial evidence surrounding what is said and done; something which non-western people, such as Middle Easterners, are able to bring to the text, for the illumination of westerners.[2]

Creation

On creation morning, God is referred to as *elohim*, a Hebrew word in the plural form. It reflects a consultation that takes place during which *elohim* said: 'Let *us* make human beings in *our* image, in *our* likeness' (Gen. 1:26, italics mine). The consistent use of this plural form suggests that it is both intentional and necessary to describe the corporate activity that was going on. The Qur'an also uses the plural form to refer to God, but this is simply a convention of classical Arabic which is akin to the 'royal we' – a device that indicates respect for the deity, while rejecting the idea of plurality in the deity.

In the New Testament the Creator is identified as being Jesus Christ, in whom 'all things were created: things in heaven and on earth, visible and invisible . . . all things have been created through him and for him . . . and in him all things hold together' (Col. 1:16–17). The writer of the letter to the Hebrews agrees when he says:

> [God the Father] appointed [Jesus] heir of all things, and through [Jesus] also he made the universe. The Son [Jesus] is the radiance of God's glory and the exact representation of his being, sustaining all things by his powerful word (Heb. 1:2–3a).

It is important for Muslims to discover that it is the Bible – not Christians – that claims that Jesus is the creator of the universe and that he was one of the participants in that consultation about the creation of humankind (Gen. 1:26). The instances outlined below are all further examples of Jesus' eternal credentials, which can carry considerable weight with Muslims. I will follow the wording used in the Bible and use the expression 'the LORD', when referring to the pre-incarnate Christ.

The Garden of Eden

Shortly after they were created, the first man and woman, Adam and Eve, heard the voice of 'the LORD God' (i.e. *yahweh elohim*) walking in the garden during the cool breeze of the late afternoon (Gen. 3:8). The phrase 'Lord God' carries the sense '*yahweh* of God'. The fact that the LORD walked in the garden begs the question: If God is everywhere (omnipresent) and does not have a body, how could he be 'walking'? Why did the 'all-seeing' God need to call out to find out where Adam and Eve were? (Gen. 3:9) And why did they need to hide from the sight of the LORD as though he were a 'person'? (Gen. 3:10b)

The LORD who walked the Garden of Eden is unlikely to be what the New Testament refers to as 'God the Father' (Matt. 6:9; 26:39; Phil. 1:2), because he is spirit (John 1:18) and cannot be looked at by mortals due to his glory (Exod. 33:20). So it is reasonable to conclude that the 'person' walking in the garden was the pre-incarnate Christ, who came into the garden to deal face to face with the problematic creatures he had made. This challenges the Islamic view that God can never make such contact with his creation. The Bible shows the Lord not only talking with them, but serving them by making clothing from animal skins to cover them (Gen. 3:21).

After Adam and Eve's rebellion, another divine consultation took place 'among' *elohim*, after which the LORD said: 'The man has now become like one of *us*, knowing good and evil. He must not be allowed to reach . . . the tree of life . . . and live forever.' A corporate decision was made to banish them from the garden (Gen. 3:22–4).

Abraham

Later on, the LORD spoke to Abram – a key figure for Muslims – instructing him to leave his country, his ethnic clan and his extended family in order to go to an undisclosed land where, under God's blessing, he would become great, know divine protection and become the means of blessing to all nations (Gen. 12:1–3). The Qur'an's version of this promise is: 'Lo! I have appointed thee a leader [i.e. imam] for mankind' (S.2.124). Abram set out and reached Moreh where the LORD 'appeared' to him and said, 'To your offspring I will give this land.' So Abram built an altar there to 'the LORD, who had appeared to him' (Gen.12:7).

A curious episode in Abram's life was his encounter with the mysterious character Melchizedek (Gen. 14:17–20). It is not clear whether this person was an angel, a man, or our mystery visitor the LORD. The Bible suggests it was the LORD who served Abram by acting as an intermediary (intercessor) between him and the high God 'El' or '*eloah*'; the singular form of the plural '*elohim*'. Some scholars identify Melchizedek as the LORD because of the following divine indicators from elsewhere in the Bible, where he is described as:

- 'King of Righteousness' – Isaiah 32:1; Hebrews 7:1–2
- 'King of Peace' – Genesis 14:18a (*Salem* means peace); Isaiah 9:6, 7
- a Royal Priest – Genesis 14:18; Zechariah 6:13
- like the Son of God – Hebrews 4:14; 7:3
- eternal – Hebrews 7:16b, 17, 21
- custodian of an unchanging priesthood – Hebrews 7:24, 25
- the one who symbolically blessed Abram with bread and wine – Genesis 14:18
- the recipient of Abram's tithe (tenth) of the spoil.[3]

When Abram's second wife Hagar became pregnant with Ishmael, the relationships within the polygamous household became strained (Gen. 16). Abram's first wife Sarai forced Hagar to run away into the wilderness where 'the angel of the LORD' (i.e. *malach ha elohim* or the *yahweh* angel) intercepted Hagar. In Hebrew this title literally means 'The Angel [which is] the LORD'. What may help a Muslim is the fact that this phrase is consistent with other references where the Angel was clearly the LORD himself (see also Gen. 22:15–16 and 48:15–16; but notably Exod. 3:2).

Hagar encountered a 'person' who entered into conversation and exercised authority over her future (Gen. 16:10–12). Something about this person indicated to her that he was not just *from* God but *of* God, because she referred to him as divine: 'You are the God who sees me', for she said, 'I have now *seen* the One who sees me' (Gen. 16:13–14). She knew that she had met with God and survived; again the logical conclusion is that she encountered Jesus.

In Genesis 17 the LORD appeared to Abram and said, 'I am God Almighty'. An extended conversation followed during which Abram fell on his face as the LORD confirmed his covenant purpose reiterating the promise of territory for Abram's descendants and introducing the rite of circumcision and renaming him 'Abraham' (i.e. father of nations). At the end of this audience, the LORD '*went up* from [Abraham]' (v. 22, italics mine).

When Abraham was an old man, he had his last recorded encounter with 'the LORD' who was accompanied by two angels (Gen. 18) at Mamre in the foothills overlooking Sodom and Gomorrah. Abraham was sitting outside his tent in the heat of the day, when three men approached. His instinctive reaction was to offer customary Middle Eastern hospitality; failure to do so would dishonour his household. The two angels did a counter-cultural thing by asking after Abraham's wife Sarah (Gen. 18:9). Then the LORD – probably knowing she was listening – announced that he would personally instigate a pregnancy that would result in the birth of a son in her old age (i.e. Isaac). The two angels got up to go to Sodom to investigate its moral confusion (Gen. 18:16–19), when the LORD asked them: 'Shall I hide from Abraham what I am about to do? . . . For I have chosen him . . .' When the two angels had left for Sodom, Abraham remained in conversation with 'the LORD'. Some intense Middle Eastern haggling then ensued over how many innocent people might be enough to delay the annihilation of Sodom. When the LORD had finished the delicate bartering process with Abraham, he left him, presumably to return to heaven as he did not join the two angels in Sodom.

The Appearances in the Book of Exodus

Although Moses is often seen as the austere 'law-giver', his encounters with 'the LORD' in Exodus were probably more intimate and touching than those with any other person. Not only did Moses speak with the LORD 'face to face, as one speaks to a friend' (Exod. 33:11) but it was he who saw 'the form of the LORD' (Num. 12:6–8). The Qur'an refers to the incident where Moses asked God to show himself so 'that I may look upon Thee' (S.7.143). It also refers to the fact that God 'spoke to Moses directly' (S.4.164).

Exodus continues to refer to 'the LORD' as *malach ha elohim* which is a synonym of the term 'The LORD God' (i.e. *yahweh elohim*). Richard Bauckham in his book *Jesus and the God of Israel*, says:

It is difficult to separate the two. It is clear he was not a principal angel, nor was he one of the revered Patriarchs returned from the dead; nor was he some sort of subordinate deity. These options would be rejected by Jewish monotheists who would insist that all such categories would be mere 'servants' of God and not worthy of being associated with the divine identity in the way this visitor was. This has led some interpreters to conclude that 'the angel of the LORD' is the pre-incarnate Christ.[4]

In other places in Exodus the LORD is referred to as 'the Jehovah Angel' (*malach yahweh*), which can be rendered in English as 'the God Angel' (Num. 22:22, 23, 24). Elsewhere other terms are used such as 'angel of *yahweh*' (Gen. 22:11, 15–16) and even the 'messenger of the covenant' (Mal. 3:1), which is another way of saying 'angel of the covenant'. When the Bible talks about angels, the expression that is normally used is '*an* angel of the LORD', not *the* angel.

When he appeared to Moses in the burning bush, Moses was attracted not because the bush was on fire but because it was ablaze without being consumed by the fire (Exod. 3:2); an incident that is helpfully referred to in the Qur'an (S.28.30–35), which helps a Muslim find her bearings. From within the fire, the LORD identified himself as God of Abraham, Isaac and Jacob.

The Qur'an only refers to God's self-revelation in general terms, while in the Bible he explicitly identifies himself as 'I AM' (*ehyeh*) (Exod. 3:14). This literally means 'is' or 'will be', which is remarkable because the Hebrew present tense is only ever used here in this passage and it is in reference to *yahweh*. To this day, Hebrew scholars debate among themselves about the fact that the consonants YHWH seem to be made up of *haya* (was), *hova* (is) and *yihiye* (will be or is to come).

After the exodus of the Hebrew people from Egypt, the LORD was the 'Good Shepherd' to them through the wilderness for forty years, appearing to them in a pillar of cloud by day and a pillar of fire by night (Exod. 13:21). He went in front to guide them in dangerous terrain, then came behind them as a 'rear-guard' to protect them from assailants (Exod. 14:19–20). When the novelty of the exodus wore off, the Hebrews became critical and even hostile towards Moses due to their lack of water in the desert. In exasperation Moses called out to the LORD, who responded with a face-to-face meeting: 'I will *stand* there before you by the rock at Horeb' (Exod. 17:6a, italics mine). These face-to-face encounters are among the most dramatic passages in the Bible.

On one occasion God – presumably God the Father – descended on Mount Sinai in thick cloud and with a piercing trumpet blast (Exod. 19:9, 16). The mountain shook, smoked and flamed like a volcano; a scene mentioned in the Qur'an (S.7.143) which can help a Muslim. The Bible says the voice of God was heard answering Moses. Then the LORD – presumably Jesus – descended to the top of the mountain and called Moses to go up and meet him where he stood. He identified himself as the one who brought the Hebrews out of Egypt before proceeding to give Moses the Ten Commandments (Exod. 20:1–19).

God revealed his plans to Moses for the future of the Hebrew people, explaining how he would send 'an angel' before them and that the divine name of *elohim* would be 'in him' (Exod. 23:20–23). God, who will not give his glory to anyone apart from himself (Isa. 48:11), gave his glory to this angelic 'person', which suggests it is in fact 'the angel of the LORD'. The language used continues in the third person as the LORD commanded Moses to guide the Hebrew people to 'worship the LORD your God' (i.e. the Father) (Exod. 23:25a). The LORD went on to instruct Moses to do 'all that *I* say' (Exod. 23:22, italics mine). He then described how he would tend Israel like a shepherd: 'I will take away sickness from among you' (Exod. 23:25b). In Exodus 24 the LORD invited Moses to bring Aaron, Nadab, Abihu and seventy elders of Israel to come up to him on the mountain (Exod. 24:1), where they:

> saw the God of Israel. Under his feet there was something like a pavement made of lapis lazuli, as bright blue as the sky. But God did not raise his hand against these leaders of the Israelites; they saw God, and they ate and drank (Exod. 24:9–11).

I suggest that they did not die because they had actually seen Jesus, who can be seen.

In Exodus 33 Moses pitched the 'tent of meeting' some distance from the camp. Anyone who wanted to enquire of the LORD would go to the tent. When Moses went into it the pillar of cloud would come down over the entrance and the LORD would speak with Moses – presumably from the pillar of cloud. When the people saw the cloud at the entrance to the tent they stood and worshipped as the LORD spoke to Moses 'face to face, as one speaks to a friend' (v. 11).

On one occasion the LORD left the cloud and *stood* at the entrance to the tent in person to reprimand Aaron and Miriam for disrespecting Moses (Num. 12:5). Moses' conversation with the LORD in Exodus 33 became increasingly intimate, to the point where Moses asked the LORD to show him the glory of God Almighty. The LORD said, 'I will cause all my goodness to pass in front of you, and I will proclaim my name, the LORD, in your presence . . . But . . . you cannot see my face, for no one may see me and live' (Exod. 33:18–20).

When Moses broke the stone tablets of the law in anger (Exod. 32), he was invited to go back up Mount Sinai to receive a second copy (Exod. 34), which he got when the LORD descended to the top of the mountain in a cloud of glory for a second time, to 'stand' next to Moses. The text becomes less clear: 'And he passed in front of Moses, proclaiming, "the LORD, the LORD, the compassionate and gracious God . . ."' Moses bowed down to the ground in worship – a posture used by Orthodox Christians and Muslims alike – and asked, 'Lord, if I have found favour in your eyes, then let the Lord go with us' (Exod. 34:9). This suggests that Moses asked the LORD God Almighty (i.e. the Father) for permission to have the LORD (i.e. Jesus) stay with them on their wilderness wanderings.

The Appearances in the Book of Judges

In Judges 2, the 'angel of the LORD' travelled from Gilgal to Bokim in order to announce to 'all the Israelites' that it was he who had spoken to Abraham, Isaac and Jacob; it was he who had rescued them from Egypt; and it was he who had given them the land they now occupied. He went on to castigate them for disobeying him. It is remarkable that the people recognized who he was, which prompted corporate weeping – which is the meaning of '*bokim*' – and the offering of sacrifices to him.

In Judges 6 the angel of the LORD appeared as a man and 'sat down under the oak' where Gideon was threshing wheat. The LORD entered into conversation with Gideon – just as he did much later in the New Testament with the Samaritan woman at the well (John 4). Like the woman, Gideon was soon unburdening himself to the

LORD about the state of the nation of Israel, but the angel of the LORD went on to commission him to go and do something about it. Gideon instinctively recognized that he was in the presence of divinity, so he asked the LORD for a sign that it was really him. There was a pause in the proceedings while Gideon prepared a roasted meal as an offering, which the LORD told Gideon to put on a rock and touch it with his staff. As he did so the meat was consumed by fire that emanated from the rock. At this point the LORD disappeared into the fire as he had done at the burning bush in Exodus 3. After the angel had gone, Gideon cried out, 'Ah, Sovereign LORD!' (i.e. apparently referring to God the Father), 'I have seen the angel of the LORD face to face!' Then Gideon received the answer, 'Do not be afraid. You are not going to die.'

In Judges 13, Israel was in moral decline, and vulnerable to Philistine harassment. The angel of the LORD appeared to a woman who is identified as the wife of Manoah – which is typical in male-orientated societies. The woman is suffering the social stigma of childlessness, yet it is to her that the angel of the LORD came with an 'annunciation' of a supernatural birth (see Gen. 18:10 and Luke 1:26–38). The LORD told her she would become pregnant with a son – Samson – who would be the next judge (i.e. *mishpat* or justice-bringer) who would deliver Israel from the Philistines. The woman reported this to her husband Manoah, referring to him as 'a man of God' who 'looked like an angel' and was 'very awesome' but he 'didn't tell me his name.' When the LORD returned, Manoah – like Jacob before him – requested to know the name of the visitor. The LORD said his name was *peleh* (i.e. hidden or beyond understanding);[5] a word which is rendered elsewhere as 'wonderful' (Isa. 9:6).

The Appearances in the First Book of Chronicles

When King David was incited by the devil to hold a census of all fighting men in the Israelite army (1 Chr. 21), the LORD was offended and sent the prophet Gad to inform David that Israel would be judged for this action. David was offered three possible ways for this guilt to be removed – a three-year famine, to be left at the mercy of his enemies, or to 'fall into the hands of the LORD'. David chose to fall into the LORD's hands, so a three-day plague erupted, killing 70,000 men at the hands of a destroying angel who attacked Jerusalem. When the LORD had seen enough he commanded the destroying angel to stop. The 'angel of the LORD was then seen, standing at the threshing-floor of Araunah the Jebusite' (1 Chr. 21:15) where he was 'standing between heaven and earth with a drawn sword in his hand extended over Jerusalem' (v. 16). At this point, David repented confessing his fault in front of the elders; a humble example to set in a position-orientated society. David prayed to the 'angel of the LORD' calling him 'LORD my God' (v. 17) before building an altar and worshipping the LORD. David was so shaken by the encounter that he was afraid to go too close because of the sword being brandished by 'the angel of the LORD' (1 Chr. 21:30).

The Appearance to the Prophet Daniel

King Nebuchadnezzar violated the human rights of his people by legalizing idolatry and insisting that the public should 'fall down and worship' a statue, probably of himself (Dan. 3:6). The penalty for non-compliance was death by burning, which prompted a crisis of conscience for the monotheistic Jewish community. Three young Jews, Shadrach, Meshach and Abednego, were reported to the king for non-compliance and sentenced to death in the furnace, which was heated to seven times the normal temperature. The three young men were tied up and thrown into the furnace where a fourth person was seen 'walking around in the fire, unbound and unharmed'. The king described the fourth person as 'like a son of the gods' (Dan. 3:25). He seemed to assume it was an angel (Dan. 3:28). When the three Jews were brought out, they were not even singed. This intervention by the angel of the LORD was necessary, not just because of the showdown with the powers that be, but because the survival of the Jewish nation may have been at stake, making this a milestone in Jewish history and in God's purposes to bless humanity as promised through Abraham's lineage (Gen. 12:1–3).

In chapter 7, Daniel had a prophetic dream about four beasts, which were a visual representation of future eras of human history. The climax of the dream was a glimpse of the Last Day – known to Muslims as Judgement Day (*yawm uddin*) (S.2.62) – when multitudes will be gathered before God and the books of judgement will be opened. In Daniel's dream the LORD of history appeared and took the judgement seat. He was referred to as the 'Ancient of Days' (Dan. 7:9). Then 'one like a son of man (i.e. Jesus) was seen coming with the clouds of heaven' to interact with the Ancient of Days (i.e. the Father). Daniel saw this 'person' led into the presence of the Ancient of Days where:

he was given authority, glory and sovereign power; all nations and peoples of every language worshipped him. His dominion is an everlasting dominion that will not pass away, and his kingdom is one that will never be destroyed (Dan. 7:13–14).

The Lord also made appearances to Jacob, Joshua, Solomon, Elijah, Isaiah and Ezekiel, as well as being featured in the book of Psalms. For the sake of brevity I have included these in Appendix A for readers who want to explore these visitations further. While this summary is not exhaustive, it is nevertheless crucial to an eastern reading of the Bible, where Jesus is centre-stage and active throughout the Old Testament as a member of *elohim* who is involved in the world he made.

We move next to the final, longest and most significant visit of 'the LORD', when he came in flesh and blood and lived among us as Messiah, for thirty-three years. We will examine Jesus' birth, teaching and miracles; all of which carried the hallmarks of divinity, the foundation to an eastern telling of the gospel.

An eastern telling of the gospel – helpful hint No. 2

Islam teaches that God cannot come into direct contact with his creation. However, the Qur'an refers to Jesus as the 'Word of God' (S.3.39, 45; 4.171), a title that is evidently taken from the Bible (John 1:1–14; Rev. 19:13). The Bible seems to show a link between the title 'Word of God' and the fact that:

- Elohim *spoke* creation into being by a word. For example, 'Let there be light, and there was light' (Gen. 1:3; see also vv. 6, 9, 11, 14, 20, 24).
- Adam and Eve 'heard the *sound* of the LORD [*elohim*] as he was walking in the garden' (Gen. 3:8), an apparent reference to the physical presence on

> earth of the pre-incarnate Christ who came to earth to deal face to face with his problematic creatures.
> - New Testament writers identify Jesus as the one 'through whom also he [God] made the universe' (Heb. 1:2–3).
> - Several people – such as Moses – spoke with the LORD (Jesus) 'face to face, as one speaks to a friend' (Exod. 33:11). Moses also saw 'the form of the LORD' (Num. 12:6–8).

If 'the LORD' is Jesus then we can heed the words of his mother, Mary, who said, 'Do whatever he tells you' (John 2:1–11). Among his instructions are the words, 'Come to me . . . and I will give you rest' (Matt. 11:28).

Notes

[1] Blamires, Harry, *The Christian Mind – How Should a Christian Think?* (Ann Arbor: Servant Books, 1978).

[2] Hollenweger, Walter, *Intercultural Theology*, in *Theological Renewal*, No. 10, ed. Thomas A. Smail, October 1978 (Fountain Trust), pp. 2–14.

[3] Goldsmith, Martin, *Matthew and Mission – the Gospel through Jewish Eyes* (Carlisle: Paternoster, 2001), p. 24.

[4] Bauckham, Richard, *Jesus and the God of Israel: God Crucified and Other Studies on the New Testament's Christology of Divine Identity* (Milton Keynes: Paternoster, 2008).

[5] Taine, Paul, *King of the Jews* (London: Lakeland, 1969).

5.

Jesus in the New Testament

If you think you can't share the gospel without John 3:16 then you don't know the gospel.

Colin Bearup[1]

Throughout his Old Testament visits, Jesus seemed to have a supernatural body in which he could appear or disappear, enter fire and hover in thin air or cloud. However, the incarnation confined him to the vulnerability of the human condition, except for sickness and sinfulness. The prophet Isaiah described his birth as the unveiling of the 'glory of the Lord' (Isa. 40:5) and the hymn writer Charles Wesley wrote: 'Veiled in flesh the Godhead see! Hail the incarnate Deity! Pleased as man with man to dwell, Jesus our Immanuel' (i.e. 'God with us').

In this chapter I have chosen, where possible, to look at Jesus' earthly experience through the account of Matthew's Gospel. This is the most Semitic of the four gospels and is therefore more eastern in mindset, which helps demonstrate for a Muslim, Jesus' divine credentials.[2]

Jesus' Genealogy

A genealogy is a badge of authenticity in eastern societies, which is why they are important to Muslims. Jesus' genealogy was recorded by Matthew and Luke, though Jewish and Muslim people may appreciate more the Semitic edge in Matthew's version because, while Luke takes Jesus' line back to Adam, showing Jesus' humanity (Luke 3:23–38), Matthew parses up the generations into three groups of fourteen. This reflects the fact that in Judaism the number seven indicates deity, as reflected in aspects of the tabernacle in the wilderness – the most obvious being the seven-branched candlestick. It is no coincidence, therefore, that Matthew displays Jesus' genealogy in three groups of fourteen (i.e. double sevens).

He also traces Jesus' line back through King David (i.e. the royal household) to Abraham (father of the spiritual household): 'This is the genealogy of Jesus the Messiah the son of David, the son of Abraham' (Matt. 1:1–17). Rahab the prostitute and Ruth the Moabitess – both Gentile outsiders – are included in Matthew's genealogy, which shows Jesus to be the final fulfilment of the original promise that he himself had made to Abraham to bless the Gentile nations (Gen. 12:3b; 22:18). So Matthew's Jewish genealogy makes it clear that the Gentile blood of the nations was flowing in the veins of Messiah as he shed his blood to redeem the nations.[3]

Jesus' Birth

Jesus' birth was unique among all the prophets in that it was accompanied by a flurry of angelic activity including the annunciation by Gabriel to Mary (Luke 1:26–38;

see also the Qur'an S.3.42). Many Muslims are already aware that the Qur'an teaches that Jesus' conception was supernatural and that he was the son of a virgin (S.19.16–33; 4.156).

Other angelic appearances around Jesus' birth include Joseph's dream where he was instructed to continue in his fragile plans to marry Mary (Matt. 1:20); another warning was given to Joseph in a dream, which took him and Mary and the Christ-child to Egypt for safety until the death of Herod. In yet another dream, Joseph was alerted that it was safe to return to Israel (Matt. 2:13–15, 19).

The promised Christ-child was to be a boy and he was to be called *yeho-shua* ('Joshua' in Hebrew and 'Jesus' in Greek), which literally means '*yahweh* saves'. The name 'Jesus' was common at the time, but the angel was emphatic that he should be called Jesus '*because* he will save his people from their sins' (Matt. 1:21–22, italics mine); in other words, Jesus is *yahweh*, saving us.

> We observe, therefore, that the ministry of Jesus in saving from sin is equated with the work of YHWH himself. The emphasis on 'he' in Matthew 1:21 underlines the fact that Jesus is not just the instrument of YHWH in this work of salvation, but rather it is he himself who fulfils this task. There is no distinction between 'YHWH saves' and 'Jesus saves'. Jesus is YHWH incarnate.[4]

Muslims may be struck by the fact that Jesus' birth was accompanied by a string of supernatural events in the cosmos. Even in the Qur'an, Jesus' birth was a 'miraculous sign for all people' (S.21.91). The Bible seems to allude to the stellar display that surrounded the Nativity as told by Matthew 2:1–12. The European Space Agency asserts that the star of Bethlehem was likely to have been a succession of astronomical events including a super-nova, a comet, and a 'broom star'. Remember that, in the ancient world, static and moving stars (i.e. planets) were seen as the same thing.[5]

Jesus was born in the constellation of Pisces and Aries (commonly identified with the Jews and Israel). The indications were that there was going to be a change of ruler in Israel, which is why magi were searching for the 'King of the Jews' (Matt. 2:2). They were alerted by the highly unusual planetary alignment that took place between Jupiter and Saturn, which formed a double act that is seen once in a millennium. It is visible from the earth because the earth orbits the sun faster than most other planets. When this alignment happens, Jupiter and Saturn appear to stop and travel backwards for about one hundred days; they then stop again, change directions and resume their journey together across the night sky – a phenomenon known as 'retrograde motion'.[6]This would explain why the star of Bethlehem appeared to stop and then move on (Matt. 2:9). The significance of all this is that the cosmos itself attended to the needs of its Creator as the alignment of Jupiter and Saturn guided the magi the last five miles from Jerusalem to Bethlehem (Matt. 2:11). The word 'magi' is the source of the word 'magician'. The ancient Jewish philosopher Philo described them as follows:

> Among the Persians there is the Order of the Magi who silently make research into the facts of nature to gain knowledge of the truth; and through visions clearer than speech, give and receive the revelations of divine excel-lency.[7]

The Persian 'Order of the Magi' was an astronomical fel-lowship. They may even have been Zoroastrians, which was the predominant religion of the Persian Empire. Zoroastrianism, like Judaism, believes in one God and a Messiah figure inspired by the prophecy of Daniel (Dan. 2:48; 5:11; 6:3). This later became a tenet of *shi'ite* Islam in Iran (i.e. modern Persia) where this Islamic messianic figure is called the *mahdi*. The Zoroastrian science of astrology created horoscopes and expected to be able to foretell significant events such as the birth and death of kings.

The account of the visit of the magi to the Christ-child uses the word 'worship' (*proskuneo*) three times (Matt. 2:1–2, 8, 11a). This seems to indicate the presence, not just of royalty, but divinity. The magi's gifts of gold, frankincense and myrrh were all significant (Matt. 2:11); for example, gold reflected divinity and was used for the fixtures and fittings of the Jewish temple which were overlaid with gold, reflecting its association with worship (1 Kgs. 6:19–30; 1 Chr. 18). Frankincense was appropriate for doing obeisance to a king, while myrrh was used to mourn royalty and to embalm them in death. Jesus is the God-man who was born to die.

Jesus the Fulfilment of Prophecy

Jesus taught that the Old Testament writings of *torah*, the prophetic tradition and the wisdom literature 'testify about me' (John 5:39). His life fulfilled everything that had been 'said through the prophet' (Matt. 1:22). On the road to Emmaus, Jesus talked his travel companions through the entire Jewish Scriptures, which must have included the material we have looked at so far about Jesus' pre-incarnate activity.

How foolish you are and how slow to believe all that the prophets have spoken! . . . And beginning with Moses and all the Prophets, he explained to them what was said in all the Scriptures concerning himself (Luke 24:25–27).

As a guest in a local synagogue, Jesus was handed the Old Testament scrolls and invited to read the appointed text for the day, a significant messianic text from Isaiah 61, which Jesus applied to himself:

'The Spirit of the Lord is on me, because he has anointed me to proclaim good news to the poor . . . freedom for the prisoners . . . recovery of sight for the blind . . . set the oppressed free . . . proclaim the year of the Lord's favour.'[He then sat down and said,] 'Today this scripture is fulfilled in your hearing.' (Luke 4:17–21)

Jesus accepted Worship

In eastern cultures there are differing degrees of worship, from the human to the divine: for example, the obeisance given to religious clerics such as Orthodox clergy or a Muslim *sheikh*. The higher the person's rank, the more pronounced the ritual of bowing to the height of their waist and attempting to kiss their hand (or ring, in the case of a bishop). The holy man pulls his hand away in a show of humility while the person honouring him tries to follow it to plant the intended kiss. This behaviour is actually a sub-set of worship.

However, this is mere deference at the human level to satisfy social convention. The Jews in Jesus' day – and Muslim people today – all know that true worship is reserved for God alone. Yet the word repeatedly used about Jesus is the Greek word *proskuneo*, which goes beyond reverential respect to adoration. For example, the gospels say he was not only 'worshipped' by the magi (Matt. 2:11); but also a leprosy sufferer (Matt. 8:2); a synagogue attendant (Matt. 9:18); a desperate house-wife (Matt. 15:25) and the disabled (John 9:38). Jesus accepted worship from Mary Magdalene and other women (Matt. 28:9); Thomas the doubter (John 20:28) and from his disciples just before his ascension (Matt. 28:17). Most of these worshippers would be well aware of the Old Testament's uncompromising position that only God can be worshipped (Exod. 34:14; Deut. 6:13). When people tried to worship the first apostles they were reminded that they too were only men (Acts 10:25–26). Nevertheless, early Christians quickly linked Jesus to divinity and openly declared him to be God in the flesh (Col. 1:18b; Heb. 1:6b).

The Miracles of Jesus

So prolific was Jesus' healing work, the Qur'an refers to his healing of 'those born blind, and the lepers and I quickened the dead' (S.3.49). Muslims also refer to Jesus as 'the healing prophet' based on Sura 5.110. The gospel for Muslims therefore points Muslims to the material in the four Gospels where the scant details about Jesus in the Qur'an is taken from. Healing was so central to the activity of Messiah, the prophet Isaiah described him as the one who would 'take up our pain' and 'bear our suffering' (Isa. 53:4; Matt. 8:17; 1 Pet. 2:24).[8]

When he arrived, this took on stunning proportions as Jesus issued imperative commands and things happened (Matt. 8:16): 'Be clean' (Matt. 8:3); 'Go!' and a servant was healed instantly (Matt. 8:13); 'Quiet! Be still!' and the sea became calm (Mark 4:39); 'Be opened!' and the deaf heard (Mark 7:34) and 'Be quiet! Come out!' and demons departed (Mark 1:25).

Jesus also issued destructive words of judgement, for example where he cursed a fig tree for not having fruit in season (Matt. 21:18–22). Many Muslims understand 'curse' to be a negative form of blessing, a sort of 'anti-blessing'; a belief especially held in the animistic parts of the world where supernatural power is seen as being like electricity, which can be channelled either positively (i.e. to give light) or negatively (to electrocute). For instance, when Jesus cursed the cities of Korazin and Bethsaida for unbelief, destruction eventually came, years after this word was spoken (Matt. 11:21–23).

> An interesting example of the authority of [Jesus] the Speaking One has been found through archaeological excavations. In New Testament times, Tiberias, Korazin, Bethsaida and Capernaum were four major towns round the Sea of Galilee. Today, Tiberias remains a thriving town but Korazin has been a ruin since the fourth century, Capernaum was levelled by an earthquake in AD 746 and was never rebuilt, and Bethsaida was so utterly destroyed by successive earthquakes that it was only discovered in 1988. Why were those three in particular so decimated? Because the one who speaks with authority said: 'Woe to you Korazin! And woe to you Bethsaida! . . . And you Capernaum, will you be lifted up to the skies? No, you will go down to the depths.'[9]

We have seen that the cosmos was set in motion by Jesus, the creative Word of God, who also upholds by his power what he has made (Heb. 1:3).[10] It should not surprise us to discover that when he came into this world 'he should behave like he owned the place' as someone put it. The truth of the matter is that Jesus did such miracles because he is *yahweh*, who alone has sovereign authority over 'everything' (Ps. 8:6; Matt. 12:27; Heb. 1:8–9).

A miracle is simply the overriding of the laws of nature. Jesus explained their occurrence as follows: 'The Father loves the Son and has placed everything in his hands' (John 3:35). In other words Jesus claimed – both implicitly and explicitly – to hold sovereign power over the universe.[11] It is little wonder that his public displays of authority covered every area of creation – i.e. the natural world, the demonic world, sin, death and coming judgement. These issues seem to be specially selected to speak eloquently about Jesus' divinity.

Jesus' authority

. . . *over the physical world*

The Gospels highlight Jesus' authority over the elements. These events intentionally paralleled their Old Testament equivalents – particularly where Moses and Elijah were involved. For example, Jesus' power over water where he stilled a storm (Matt. 8:23–27), walked on water (Matt. 14:22–33), and turned water into wine (John 2:1–11). These actions paralleled Moses at the Red Sea (Exod. 14) and are reminiscent of the Nile being turned into blood, then back into water (Exod. 7:14–24).

Jesus demonstrated power over the physical world when he supernaturally landed a huge haul of fish by contradicting the conventional wisdom of the fishing industry (Luke 5:1–11). This event paralleled the provision of the quail under Moses in the wilderness (Exod. 16). Jesus multiplied fish and bread to feed a crowd of 5,000 men (not including women and children) (John 6). This paralleled Moses' provision of 'manna from heaven' (Exod. 16); a sign that Jesus was the Creator at work – an unmistakable manifestation of deity.

... *over demons*

Muslims believe in demons more readily than many westerners. Jesus demonstrated absolute authority over them. His first challenge from the demonic realm came in his temptation in the wilderness (Matt. 4), where the devil himself urged Jesus to throw himself from a great height. He quoted Psalm 91:11–12. '[God] will command his angels concerning you and they will lift you up in their hands, so that you will not strike your foot against a stone' (Matt. 4:6). The devil stopped quoting just before the psalm says: 'You will tread on the lion and the cobra; you will trample the great lion and the serpent' (Ps. 91:13). The reason may have been that this prophetic imagery shows the believer's authority over Satan (Gen. 3:1–7; Rev. 9:1–11, 19; 12:9; Luke 10:19).

Jesus demonstrated this 'trampling' of Satan when he exorcised a whole community of demons that was living in a man called Legion. The demons were ordered into a herd of pigs which were not supposed to be kept on Jewish soil anyway (Matt. 8:28–34). Jesus also drove out a blind and mute spirit from a man so that he could both see and speak (Matt. 12:22–32). At Jesus' word, demons came out shrieking as they left. One demon even came out yelling: 'You are the Son of God!' (Luke 4:41).

... *over sin*

When Jesus was presented with a sick man, it was implied (controversially for us perhaps) that there was a causal link between the man's sin and his sickness (Matt. 9:1–8). Jesus went further by absolving the man of whatever sin he had committed, annulling the man's status as a sinner and relieving him of the status of shame he had been assigned in the community. (This is an issue we will discuss in the third section of this book.) This provoked the religious teachers to accuse Jesus of blasphemy (Matt. 9:3); they asked, 'Who can forgive sins but God alone?' (Mark 2:7). Such forgiveness was indeed God's business, and Jesus was doing it right there in public because he was about to go to the cross in order to 'provide purification for sin' (Heb. 1:3).

As the author and giver of life (John 1:4), Jesus behaved in a manner entirely consistent with a divine identity. For example, he raised to life the daughter of Jairus, a synagogue leader (Matt. 9:18–26). This was a parallel of Elisha's raising of the Shunammite's son (2 Kgs. 4:8–37). Jesus called Lazarus out of his tomb after three days (John 11:1–44). He claimed the power to raise people from the dead (John 5:21), asserting that anyone who listens to his voice will live, both now and at the resurrection (John 5:25; 6:40). He also saw his life-giving role expanding when he promised not to lose any of those who trust him, but to raise them up on the last day (John 6:39). It is also Jesus who is the holder of 'the keys of death and Hades' (Rev. 1:18).

. . . *to judge*

Muslims believe that the knowledge of the Last Day belongs to God alone (S.41.47). This agrees with Jesus' teaching that the timing of his return is in the hands of God the Father alone (Matt. 24:36). The apostle Paul affirmed that God would judge 'everyone's secrets through Jesus Christ' (Rom. 2:16). Jesus taught that he would return in power with an army of angels, to be enthroned and have authority with God the Father, to judge nations and to separate the 'sheep' from the 'goats', based not on practising a religion but living out a relationship with him (Matt. 25:31–46). In the book of

Revelation, Jesus is identified as the One who sits on the throne to judge the living and the dead of every age (Rev. 20:11–13) – this includes people such as Guru Nanak, the Buddha and Muhammad.

Jesus' Commission to Mission

Jesus' last words on earth were: 'All authority in heaven and on earth has been given to me. Therefore go and make disciples of all nations . . . and surely I am with you always' (Matt. 28:18–20). These words carry particular resonance for Jewish people because they reflect 2 Chronicles 36:23, which happens to be the closing verse of the original Jewish Scriptures. In it, Cyrus king of Persia says:

> The LORD, the God of heaven, has given me all the kingdoms of the earth . . . Any of his people among you – may the LORD their God be with them, and let them go up.[12]

In both 2 Chronicles and the Gospel of Matthew, God promised to be with his people among the nations. Matthew encourages us to be confident about the good news of the gospel because of Jesus' presence and authority.

The Uniqueness of Jesus

Chris Wright points out that it is better not to compare Jesus horizontally with other people such as the Buddha or Muhammad, but rather to compare him vertically with God because he is in a league of his own. All other figures of history pale into insignificance on a vertical comparison with Jesus the Lord.[13]

But why, some ask, did Jesus never come out and say plainly that he was God? The answer is simple: instead of blurting out 'I am God!' Jesus consistently did exactly what the Old Testament said would happen when 'the LORD' comes among humanity. For example, the blind would see, the deaf would hear, the lame would leap and the mute would shout out for joy (Isa. 35:2, 5–6). The apostle Paul made one of the clearest declarations of his deity when he quoted the 'kenotic hymn' (i.e. song of emptying) that was used in the early church to celebrate *elohim's* cooperation to divest himself of divine privilege, in order to redeem humankind:

> God exalted [Jesus] to the highest place and gave him the name that is above every name, that at the name of Jesus every knee should bow, in heaven and on earth and under the earth, and every tongue acknowledge that Jesus Christ is Lord, to the glory of God the Father (Phil. 2:9–11).

These words are rooted in the messianic prophecy of Isaiah: 'By myself I have sworn ... before me every knee will bow; by me every tongue will swear' (Isa. 45:23). So Jesus Christ was 'God with his sleeves rolled up', who came among us to save us.

Having seen that Jesus' incarnation was – in all likelihood – the longest of a series of visits that had gone on through the Old Testament era, it seems clear that through this process, the LORD was edging ever closer to humankind until the point where he miraculously became one of us.

But why did people who met Jesus, sense that he was not just 'from' *elohim* but that he was actually 'of' *elohim*? What do we mean by 'the divine name' and what do we mean when we say that Jesus is a participator in the divine name? These are issues that bring us to the heart of the gospel for Muslims. The material in the next chapter may be shocking for many Muslims but it points to a very unexpected answer to their most profound predicament.

Notes

[1] Bearup, Colin, *A Set of Keys – Opening up the Gospel for Muslims using Matthew's Gospel* (Bulstrode: WEC Publications, 2009), p. 6.

[2] Neyrey, Jerome, H., *Honor and Shame in the Gospel of Matthew* (Louisville: Westminster John Knox Press, 1998), p. 90.

[3] Piper, John, *A Sweet and Bitter Providence – Sex, Race and the Sovereignty of God* (Wheaton: Crossway Books, 2010).

[4] Goldsmith, Martin, *Matthew and Mission – the Gospel through Jewish Eyes* (Carlisle: Paternoster, 2001), p. 13.

[5] The BBC2 programme *Star of Bethlehem*, screened on 24 December, 2008.

[6] The Chinese Han Shu record of stellar activity on the same latitude as the Holy Land was begun 200 years before Christ. This star lasted seventy days.

[7] The BBC2 programme *Star of Bethlehem*, screened on 24 December, 2008.

[8] Petts, David, the conclusion of a PhD thesis on the subject of healing.

[9] Wilson, Andrew, *Incomparable* (Eastbourne: Kingsway/Survivor, 2007).

[10] Tozer, A.W., *The Knowledge of the Holy* (Carlisle: STL Publishing, 1987), p. 91.

[11] Raymond, Ronald, *Jesus Divine Messiah: The New Testament Witness* (Phillipsburg: Presbyterian and Reformed, 1990), pp. 121–2.

[12] Goldsmith, Martin, *Matthew and Mission – the Gospel through Jewish Eyes* (Carlisle: Paternoster, 2001), p. 207.

[13] Wright, Christopher J.H., *The Mission of God – Unlocking the Bible's Grand Narrative* (Leicester: Inter-Varsity Press, 2006).

6.

Jesus' True Identity

'Isaiah saw Jesus' glory and spoke about him.'

John 12:41

I have never yet met a Muslim who has a problem referring to Jesus as God's Word incarnate (S.3.39) nor a
Muslim that does not accept that the Qur'an talks about
Jesus: 'proceeding from God' (S.4.171). The prophet
Micah said of Messiah: His *'goings forth* have been from
of old, from everlasting' (Mic. 5:2, italics mine). When a
Muslim can hold these two thoughts of Jesus' eternity
and his title 'Word of God' together, the words of the
apostle John can become extremely potent for them:

> *In the beginning* was the Word, and the Word was with God,
> and the Word was God . . . Through him all things were
> made; without him nothing was made that has been made
> . . . The Word became flesh and made his dwelling among
> us (John 1:1–14a).

More enquirers from Muslim backgrounds, than at any
time in church history, are putting these two issues
together and finding that they want to take the step of
accepting that 'the Word' *is* in fact God. This is the same

discovery that early Jewish followers of Jesus had to make. Their problem was the same as a modern Muslim – how can a man be God?

When Jesus arrived as Messiah it was like a theological bomb going off, which blew apart the traditional Jewish expectation. Opinions about Jesus were therefore divided with many Jews reacting strongly against him – just as many Muslims do today. The Jews seemed to forget their Old Testament in order to protect their tradition. They went on the offensive to denounce the claim that God was among them, branding any who believed in Jesus as 'blasphemers' – as do most Muslims.

On the other hand, other equally monotheistic Jews were quickly satisfied that Jesus was indeed God in the flesh and that he was to be included in the 'divine name' of *elohim*. In fact the Jews who met Jesus in both the Old and New Testaments recognize who he was. If this could happen to monotheistic Jews, it can also happen to Muslims who must account for the Qur'an's references, which imply that Jesus is divine. For example, while Moses is referred to as *kallimullah* (the one to whom God spoke; S.4.164), Jesus was referred to as *kalimatullah* (word from/of God; S.3.39, 45; 4.171). And this is what we are seeing today as unprecedented numbers of Muslims are turning to Jesus. Monotheists can and do embrace Jesus as a member of the Godhead.

When I lived in the Middle East, I undertook some postgraduate research in Applied Linguistics. I was impacted by the work of Denis Alexander, who highlighted the fact that a word is inseparable from the person who utters it. It is a product of the speaker's past, their personality and their mind. To speak a word involves the use of over two hundred muscles in the diaphragm, chest, neck and face, and the word is given expression upon the exhaled breath (i.e. spirit) of the speaker.[1] Modern technology has found a unique 'sound trace' in the human voice which, when recorded, enables a more accurate identification than a fingerprint, and so can be used as evidence against suspected criminals. So to refer to Jesus as 'the Word of God' means he is indistinguishable from *elohim*, because he is part of *elohim*.

So if a Muslim is going to reject the Trinity, it is better that they reject the real definition of it, rather than the bizarre versions they hear i.e. that it is three gods, or even a 'three-headed god', as one Muslim cleric put it to me.

Jesus – the Word of God in the Flesh

Whatever supernatural form 'the LORD' took on his brief visits in the Old Testament, when he entered the human race as Messiah, he took on the human condition. Followers of Jesus down the centuries have wrestled with the seeming impossibility that Jesus could be both God and man; this was particularly so during the first 400 years of church history, where three main views vied for acceptance.

1. **Docetism** – a belief influenced by Greek thought, where Jesus came to earth as 'all divine', but only 'appeared' to be human (Greek: *dokein*).
2. **Ebionitism** – a belief influenced by strict Jewish thought, where Jesus came to earth as 'all man', with deity somehow bestowed on him at his baptism.
3. **Arianism** – the belief that Jesus' humanity was enhanced by divinity, which was only 'immanent' in him but not fully incarnated.

Like views 1 and 2, Arianism struggled with the Biblical fact that divinity was fully 'incarnated' into the human condition.

At the Council of Chalcedon (AD 451) bishops and theologians agreed that Jesus was both fully man and fully God. This is by no means a solution to the mystery, but rather a definition of the tension to be maintained. The debate has rumbled on through the Reformation to this day, but the Chalcedon statement continues to be the starting point for orthodox belief in, and debate about, Jesus the 'God-man'.

This tension is described – though not explained – by the apostle Paul who included Jesus in the triune God when he described him as God in 'very nature' (i.e. *huparchon*; Phil. 2:6). Paul went on to say that Jesus also took on himself the 'very nature' of a servant and was 'made in human likeness' (i.e. *morphe*; 'became in nature' or 'transitioned to'; Phil. 2:7). Elsewhere Paul says: 'in Christ all the fullness of the deity lives in bodily form' (Col. 2:9). Jesus is also described as the 'radiance of God's glory and the exact representation of his being' (Heb. 1:3) and the 'image of the invisible God' (Col. 1:15). The meaning here is that of the image of a monarch on a coin that is pressed into the clay of human flesh leaving the perfect imprint in the clay. The following features describe the imprint of Jesus' divinity during his earthly human life.

Jesus was sinless

Jesus confidently asserted his sinlessness when he asked, 'Can any of you prove me guilty of sin?' (John 8:46). The apostle Peter said 'he *committed* no sin' (1 Pet.

2:22). The apostle Paul said 'he *had* no sin' (2 Cor. 5:21).
And the writer to the Hebrews said he was 'tempted in
every way, just as we are – yet *he did not* sin' (Heb. 4:15b).
The Qur'an referred to Jesus as *zakiyyan* or 'free of sin'
(S.3.19.19), while the following prophets were not –
Abraham (S.26.82), Moses (S.28.16) and Muhammad
(S.47.19; 48.2).[2]

Jesus transfigured

A dramatic outbreak of Jesus' divinity happened on
Mount Tabor where the apostles Peter, James and John
saw a brilliant light shining out of Jesus' body (Matt.
17:1–8). Moses and Elijah, the figureheads of the Law
and the Prophets, appeared and talked with Jesus.
Reporting this event as an older man, Peter – who had
spent quality time with Jesus – said, 'We were eyewit-
nesses of his majesty' (2 Pet. 1:16). The apostle John did
the same when he said 'We have seen his glory, the glory
of the one and only Son, who came from [God] the
Father' (John 1:14).

Jesus cannot be separated from the Law and the
Prophets because he was the author and inspiration of
both. The law of Moses was given by Jesus: '[Moses]
wrote about me . . .' (John 5:46); likewise the prophets
were inspired by the 'Spirit of Christ' who was speaking
through them (1 Pet. 1:11). Jesus taught that he was
greater than all – Moses, the prophets and even the temple itself (Matt. 12:6, 41, 42).

Another indicator of Jesus' inclusion in *elohim* is the
fact that, in non-western cultures, a person's identity is
bound up in their name. We have seen that Jesus' true
identity was kept hidden when Jacob asked him for his
name (Gen. 32:29); when Manoah asked, he was told

clearly that it was *peleh* (hidden) or 'beyond understanding' (Judg. 13:17–18). This Hebrew word is linked to the word 'wonderful', which was one of the titles of the Messiah who would be: 'Wonderful Counsellor' (Isa. 9:6).[3] The apostle John in the book of Revelation also found that Jesus had a name that was 'known only to himself' (Rev. 19:12).

We are brought a step closer to knowing Jesus' hidden name through his nature, written on him as the names 'Faithful' and 'True'. He is the one who will ultimately bring justice to the earth (Rev. 19:11).

Jesus' Death and Resurrection

The apostle Paul said: 'he was appointed the son of God in power by his resurrection from the dead' (Rom. 1:4). When he was raised from the dead, his 'resurrection body' had changed from what it was prior to the crucifixion. The renewed resurrection body enabled him to move freely and in different guises, probably as he had done in the Old Testament visits before he was restricted by his incarnation. For example, he appeared to various believers over a forty-day period (Acts 1:3); he appeared to people in locked rooms (John 20:26; Acts 23:11); he appeared and disappeared at will to the twelve disciples (Luke 24:31); he appeared – apparently in mid-air – to Saul of Tarsus (Acts 9:3–4). His resurrection body was not immediately recognizable, even to Mary Magdalene outside his tomb (John 20:10–16); neither did his disciples recognize him when he appeared to them back in Galilee (John 21:4–7).

Jesus as God – Continuity of Language

Yet another indicator that Jesus is part of the plural divine name of God, is the terminology that is carried on from the Old Testament and into the New Testament, where Jesus is consistently recognized as being a participant with the Father in the divine identity.[4] This was possible because Jews recognized that the arrival of the Messiah would be, in some special way, the arrival of God on earth. This enabled the early church to assert that 'Jesus is LORD' (i.e. Jesus is *yahweh*); this carried political connotations which led to them facing death in the coliseums, as traitors to Caesar.

Many Muslims will be struck by the fact that the apostle Paul, as a converted rabbi from a strict monotheistic background, refers to Jesus, using the language of deity.

> For even if there are so-called 'gods', whether in heaven or on earth (as indeed there are many 'gods' and many 'lords'), yet for us there is but one God, the Father, from whom all things came and for whom we live; and there is but one Lord, Jesus Christ, through whom all things came and through whom we live (1 Cor. 8:4b–6).

In addition to Paul's dramatic encounter with the risen Christ on the Damascus Road, he would also find grounds for Jesus' divinity in the early Greek version of the Old Testament (the Septuagint) where the divine expression 'the LORD' (*ho kurios* or *yahweh*) is used 6,125 times.[5] In the New Testament, the equivalent word 'LORD' (*kurios*) is used to refer to Jesus 700 times.

Puritan divines such as John Owen and Thomas Goodwin recognized that the Old Testament mystery visitor was Jesus, referring to him as the 'divine person' or 'God-man' who 'faithfully served the needs of the people of God throughout the Old Testament'. So strong was Owen's conviction that it was Jesus, that he said only 'unbelieving Jews' would even attempt to evade the reality of the Old Testament accounts that involved him. Owen argued that they could only do so as an attempt to escape the challenging implications for their restrictive form of monotheism.

A revelation was made of a distinct person in the Deity, who in a peculiar manner managed all the concerns of the people of God after the entrance of sin into the world. The one by whom everything was made, and by whom all were to be renewed (through redemption), did in a special and glorious way, appear to Adam and Eve . . . And he appeared in human form, to instruct the Old Testament Church in the mystery of his future incarnation. He worked under the name of 'Angel of the Lord' as employed by the Father. He discovered his distinct role as the voice of the Father.[6]

Paul Blackham, a Hebrew scholar and proponent of this view, adds:

Many presentations of the gospel are basically like the Jehovah's Witnesses i.e. they treat Jesus as God's unique agent of salvation, rather than showing Jesus to be the God of Israel. I can think of many diagrams that simply identify God as the one who sends Jesus. That is okay if the biblical doctrine of God is explained at the same time, but on its own it leads to the classic problems for Muslims who are left in the situation where they never really see that it is Jesus who is in fact the God of Abraham.[7]

The Trinity

The word 'trinity' simply means 'tri-unity'. It is a truth that is revealed developmentally through the Bible; it was first coined as a theological term by the Tunisian theologian Tertullian (AD 160–225). This doctrine is based on the consistent evidence from the creation onwards that God acts as three distinct persons who are in perfect unity. Although the word 'trinity' is not found in the Bible, just as *tawhid* (the Islamic doctrine of God's oneness) is not found in the Qur'an, the concept of God as a triune being is deeply biblical.

For instance, God is referred to as 'Father' eleven times in the Old Testament and 169 times in the New Testament; he is referred to as 'Saviour' thirty-one times in the Old Testament and twenty-four times in the New Testament; and he is referred to as 'Spirit' seventy-eight times in the Old Testament and 242 times in the New Testament.

The concept of the Trinity is anathema in Islam, and most Muslims, coming from a deeply ingrained monotheistic outlook, have an instinctive reaction to the doctrine. The best help we can offer a Muslim is to explain the reasoning behind the term 'Trinity'. An important starting place is Hebrew (the language of the Old Testament) and its sister language Arabic (the language of the Qur'an). We have seen that an important Hebrew word for 'God' is *elohim*, the plural form that expresses the idea of 'compound unity'. An example of this was when Adam and Eve came together in sexual union and the two became 'one flesh' (Gen. 2:24; Matt. 19:5–6; 1 Cor. 6:16).

By contrast, the word for 'God' in Arabic is *allah*, which literally means 'the God' (n.b. a cognate of *El*); it is an expression of 'singular unity'. This difference underlies an important contrast between the theologies of Judaism, Christianity and Islam. While the oneness of God is foundational to all three theologies, the difference is that the Hebrew word for 'one' (*echad*) carries in it the idea of 'corporate oneness' as reflected in the plural name *elohim*, which messianic Jews and Muslims embrace. In contrast, the Arabic word for 'one' (*ahad*) is the root of the Arabic number one (*wahed*). This refers to a mathematical singularity, which is foundational to the Islamic doctrine of the 'oneness of God' known as *tawhid*.

When we move from 'singular unity' to 'compound unity', it is possible to understand the Bible's description of God as corporate – revealed as God Almighty (i.e. the Father), God the Word (i.e. Jesus) and the Spirit of God (i.e. the Holy Spirit). 'Compound unity' is recorded in Genesis 2 – 3, where the term 'the Lord God' literally means '*yahweh* who is [of] *elohim*'. Jesus included himself within the divine name when he used the Greek expression *ego eimi* or 'I Am' to refer to himself (Matt. 27:43; Mark 14:62). This was a direct allusion to the Old Testament where God said to Moses: 'I AM WHO I AM' (Exod. 3:14). This language was blatantly asserting that God was not just working 'in' Jesus or 'through' Jesus, but that he himself was God at work on the earth.[8]

This sort of language also challenges Muslims who understand the glory of God as something in singular isolation where God is alone, unknowable, aloof and unconnected to humankind. It therefore follows that – for Muslims – there is only room for a single 'person' in the deity. On the face of it, this seems more logical and easier to grasp. However, it can be even more problematic than a triune God because the Trinity is more practical, as illustrated by the following story told by an Australian Interserve colleague Bernie Power:

One day Ahmed fell into a hole in the desert. He was stuck until a face appeared at the top and said, 'I am alone but I will send down a book so you can work out how to rescue yourself.' Ahmad spent the rest of his life trying to climb out of the hole on his own but without success.

The next day Mabrouk fell into another hole in the desert. This time three faces appeared at the top of the hole. The first (the brave one) said, 'I'll go down if someone else (the strong one) will hold the rope for me.' The third (the gentle one) said, 'While you are doing that I'll encourage you both.' So the brave one went down and saved Mabrouk. However, while he was doing so, the hole collapsed and buried the brave one, killing him. The strong one dug and dug for three days to get him out. Meanwhile the gentle one came down the hole too and breathed life back into the brave one, and he lived again.[9]

Perhaps the question to put to a Muslim is: 'Which person would you rather be, Ahmed with a man and a book (i.e. God in singular isolation) or Mabrouk with a rescue team (i.e. God in plurality)?' As a triune being, God is able to be – at the same time – above us as the 'revealer', beside us as the 'revealed', and within us as the one inspiring 'revealedness' (i.e. revelation itself). Put another way, the triune God is able simultaneously to be the 'author', the 'implementer' and the 'applier' of salvation.

Another problem that restrictive forms of monotheism must face is that for God to *be* love there must be someone to be loved – hence a community (1 John 4:8); or as Søren Kierkegaard put it: 'Love is only comprehensible in relationship.'[10] Furthermore, the triune God provides the perfect model for interpersonal relationships in family and society – something that is depleted in Islamic politics.

A Middle Eastern commentary refers to God as 'one' in his 'creative thought (i.e. Father), his spoken word (i.e. Jesus), and his powerful Spirit'[11] while the Hebrew of the Old Testament sometimes uses several names for God in the same passage. In Genesis 1 – 3 God is referred to in the Hebrew language as *yahweh*, *adonai* and *elohim*. These three names are reflected in Psalm 38 where it says: 'LORD [*yahweh*], I wait for you. You will answer, Lord [*adonai*] my God [*elohim*]' (v. 15).

Just because the concept of the Trinity is not easy, it does not mean that it is not true. On the contrary, its complexity is also an indicator that it is describing reality. Bishop Graham Kings believes we can be confident that our understanding is not required to be 'incoherent' but 'co-inherent'.[12] By this he means that in the Bible, the Father, the Word and the Spirit are inherent in one another because they interweave like a threefold cord. This is what we find in the language used by Jesus in his Great Commission to the first apostles (Matt. 28:19).

> Jesus does not say, 'into the names (plural) of the Father and the Son and the Holy Spirit,' or what is its virtual equivalent, 'into the name of the Father, and into the name of the Son and into the name of the Holy Spirit', as if we had to deal with three separate Beings. Nor does he say 'into the name of the Father, Son and Holy Spirit' (omitting the three recurring articles), as if 'the Father, Son and Holy Ghost' might be taken as merely three designations of a single person. What he does say is this: 'into the name (singular) of *the* Father and of *the* Son, and of the Holy Spirit', first asserting the unity of the three by combining them all within the bounds of the single Name and then throwing in to emphasize the distinctiveness of each by introducing them in turn with the repeated definite article.[13]

The early church's inclusion of Jesus in the divine name of *elohim* automatically meant that they were accepting that the nature of God is a 'compound unity': 'There is but one God the Father, from whom all things came and for whom we live; and there is but one Lord, Jesus Christ, through whom all things came and through whom we live' (1 Cor. 8:6). The early church referred to the triune God in Acts 4, when they prayed to the 'Sovereign Lord' who was architect of the universe (v. 24), who spoke by the Holy Spirit (v. 25), about the Anointed One (i.e. Christ) (v. 26).

But what do we mean by the word 'divine'? The following criteria are likely to be helpful to Muslim people.

Only Deity Can Be Eternal

Only divinity can be eternal (Deut. 33:27) and so only *yahweh* can inhabit eternity (Isa. 57:15). In the Moffatt translation of the Bible, *yahweh* is used synonymously with 'the Eternal One'. God alone is 'from everlasting to everlasting' (Ps. 90:2). The Messiah is referred to as the 'Everlasting Father' (i.e. the father of the everlasting ages) with a government that will 'know no end' (Isa. 9:6–7). The writer to the Hebrews said of Jesus: 'Your throne, O God, will last for ever and ever' (Heb. 1:8). Jesus' origin was clearly outside the time/space continuum (John 1:1; 17:5), which prompted Harry Blamires to comment that he was the only person to come into the world from a prior existence.[14] This is why when Jesus talked about himself, chronology and grammatical tense became meaningless. For example, he told the Jewish religious establishment: 'Your father Abraham rejoiced at the thought of seeing my day; he saw it and was glad . . . Before Abraham was born, I am' (John 8:56–58).

Only Deity Can Create

Both Judaism and Islam agree that the ability to create something out of nothing (*ex nihilo*) or to take one form of matter (e.g. water) and transform it into another (e.g. wine) is an attribute of the divine. The prophet Isaiah declared that it is God 'who has made all things . . . stretched out the heavens and spread out the earth' (Isa. 44:24b).

The Old Testament reflects the divine longing in the heart of God that he should be known and enjoyed by his creation. This longing was only relieved as the Creator breathed his Word, exhaling that longing as the creation came into existence (Gen 2:7). We have seen that it was Jesus who was the agent of creation as well as the sustainer who holds together the atomic particles of the created order (Col. 1:16, 17, NIV). He regulates the orbital systems in the cosmos, the tides of the oceans and the seasons of the year (Heb. 1:3a). Jesus is also the ruler of creation (Acts 17:25–26), which makes him the pivotal point between the natural and the spiritual realm.

Muhammad said, 'If Allah Most Gracious had a son, I would be the first to worship' (S.43.81). On the basis of the material we have looked at so far, Muhammad had just cause to worship Jesus. If Jesus Christ is the second member of the Trinity, his death – which Muslims reject in order to protect his honour as a prophet of Islam – becomes even more significant. If the crucifixion is true, God, who does as he wills in accordance with his own divine nature, was acting like he never has done before – or since. By opting to become powerless, he overcame the powerful and by letting go of his rights, they were awarded back to him. Followers of Jesus from Christian and Muslim backgrounds celebrate him in the words of a song:

Meekness and majesty
Manhood and deity
In perfect harmony
The man who is God.
Lord of eternity
Dwells in humanity
Kneels in humility
And washes our feet.

O what a mystery
Meekness and majesty
Bow down and worship
For this is your God
This is your God.

Extract taken from the song 'Meekness and Majesty' by Graham Kendrick. Copyright © 1989 Thankyou Music.*

These words get to the nub of the problem Muslims have with Jesus being included in the divine name *elohim* – that is God embracing weakness. The idea that the indestructible God should appear in frailty and 'conquer through sacrifice'[15] is unthinkable for most Muslims because weakness and vulnerability are not Islamic values. When Muslims read the gospels they are more likely to find it easier to relate to the strident behaviour of people such as Simon Peter, who defended Jesus by taking a sword and cutting off the ear of Malchus, the high priest's servant (John 18:10); or the behaviour of the brothers James and John, who called down fire from heaven upon a community when it gave Jesus a cool reception (Luke 9:51–56). Most Muslims could not stand idly by while they, or their religion, are insulted or threatened; but why is this?

The simple answer is the DNA of Islam, which values power and prestige and discards weakness. This in turn is driven by the eastern 'honour' code, with its counterpart of 'shame'. These are two sides of the same cultural coin and are a major cause of cross-cultural misunderstanding at the political and personal level. Also, 'honour' and 'shame' form the most effective blockage to the communication of the gospel to Muslims by westerners.

The apostle Paul observed that 'Jews demand signs and Greeks look for wisdom but we preach Christ crucified: a stumbling block to Jews and foolishness to Gentiles' (1 Cor. 1:22, 23). These two categories of 'signs' (i.e. spiritual power) and 'wisdom' (i.e. human intellect) are still with us in the cultures of East/West. Muslims are like the Jews in that they seek 'signs'. I was amazed how many Muslims turned up at a meeting I attended with the German Pentecostal evangelist Reinhard Bonnke, who prays for the sick with dramatic miracles and exorcisms taking place.

So when we 'translate' the gospel for a Muslim, we need to address the issue of power, which in Muslim thinking is allied to 'honour' weakness, which is allied to 'shame'. While Muslims instinctively reject the suffering, humiliation and death of Jesus, it is ironic that Jesus himself grew up in a shame-orientated society. He intentionally submitted himself to the 'shame' of the cross, knowing that by suffering in this way, he would provide the solution to the problem of 'shame' for ever.

But what exactly do easterners mean by the terms 'honour' and 'shame'? How does their understanding differ from westerners? And how does the gospel speak into this vital issue?

An eastern telling of the gospel – helpful hint No. 3

Islam teaches that it is a blasphemous impossibility for God to have a 'son' (*walad*): 'They say: "[Allah] Most Gracious has begotten a son." Indeed you have put forth a thing most monstrous!' (S.19.88–91). 'Glory be to Him: [far Exalted is He] above having a son' (S.4.171b). '[God] begetteth not nor is he begotten' (S.112.3). The root of the Arabic word for 'son' and to 'beget' is *walada*; a term that is used to refer to human procreation.

The good news is that when the Bible calls Jesus the 'Son of God' (Isa. 9:6; Matt. 3:17; Rom. 1:3–4; Heb. 1:2, 5) and says he was 'begotten' by God, it is not insulting him by referring to him as the 'offspring' of God by a physical relationship with Mary. Rather, it is used in the sense that he and *elohim* are 'one' in the same way that someone who is never at home is called 'son of the street' because they are synonymous. Jesus and *elohim* are indistinguishable from one another as Jesus said: 'I and the Father are one' (John 10:30).

Jesus becoming 'begotten' is a reference to his physical birth in Bethlehem (Heb. 1:5; John 1:14, AV; 1 John 4:9). The title 'Son of God' is therefore a spiritual title and was never a physical description. So the claim about Jesus is not that he was '*Isa bin-allah*' (i.e. son of God by physical procreation) but '*ibn-allah*' (i.e. Son of God by his total union with him).

Notes

1. Alexander, Denis, *Beyond Science* (Oxford: Lion Publishing, 1972).
2. Al-Bukhari, *The Translation of the Meaning of Al-Bukhari*, translated by M.M. Khan, Dar Us-Sunnah, Al-Nabawiya, Vol. 9, Book 93, No. 482, pp. 358–9.
3. Taine, Paul, *King of Kings* (London: Lakeland, 1969).
4. Bauckham, Richard, *Jesus and the God of Israel – 'God Crucified' and other Studies in the New Testament's Christology of Divine Identity* (Carlisle: Paternoster, 2008), pp. 17–20.
5. *Vine's Expository Dictionary of Biblical Words* (New Haven: Thomas Nelson Publishers, 1970, 2002), p. 171.
6. Owen, John, *Commentary on the Letter to the Hebrews*, Vol. 18:216, 220. Also see Goodwin, Thomas, *The Eternal Existence of Christ Jesus* (Lafayette: Sovereign Grace Publishing, 2000).
7. Blackham, Paul, *The Gospel and Islam*, an address to a Global Connections Consultation in London, 2005.
8. Goldsmith, Martin, *Matthew and Mission – the Gospel through Jewish Eyes* (Carlisle: Paternoster, 2001), p. 207.
9. Power, Bernie, *Interserve Arab World Conference*, Holland, December 2009.
10. Graham Kings, *Signs and Seasons* (Norwich: Canterbury Press, 2008).
11. Ed. El Kacemi and Ibn Al-Arabi, cited in *The Gospel As Inspired to Saint Luke – an Eastern Reading* (Beirut: Lebanon, 1998), p. 8.
12. Graham Kings, *Signs and Seasons* (Norwich: Canterbury Press), 2008, p. 62.
13. Raymond, Ronald, *Jesus Divine Messiah: The New Testament Witness* (Phillipsburg: Presbyterian and Reformed, 1990), p. 84.
14. Blamires, Harry, *The Christian Mind – How Should a Christian Think?* (Ann Arbor: Servant Books, 1978).
15. Kendrick, Graham, *Meekness and Majesty* (copyright © 1989 Thankyou Music).

Interlude

British Muslim encounters Jesus Christ

Saira is a 33-year-old woman who was born into a Bangladeshi Muslim family and raised in the UK, where she was nurtured by her parents in the Islamic religion.

From early childhood, she became aware that God was working in her life. However, she did not change allegiance to Christ until much later in her experience when her 7-year-old daughter was healed of a rampant form of TB, while hospitalized.

This came about because Saira had asked several Christians to pray for her daughter, which they did over a two-week period. As a result of this, I had the privilege of leading Saira in a prayer of commitment of her life to Jesus Christ as her Lord and Saviour. Not only was Saira's daughter made completely healthy again, but within two months of this incident, Saira herself was sharing what had happened with other Muslim friends.

Since her conversion, Saira has been involved in Bible study with Christians and is even touching the hearts of some real western sceptics, as well as other Muslims who are being impacted by her story.

There must be many others who, like Saira, have been aware that God is at work in their lives and who are ready to respond to the gospel. These Muslim background believers can become such good witnesses to those of their own culture, as well as to others of Anglo-Saxon heritage.

A retired lady in Lancashire, 2009

Section Three:

'Shame', the Megaphone to the Muslim Heart

Interlude

An imam's daughter meets Jesus

I grew up in a town in the north of England, as the daughter of rural Pakistani parents who worked in textile factories. My father was the imam of our local mosque and lived a devout life that revolved around praying five times a day, reciting the Qur'an, preaching at the mosque and even travelling to other UK towns for religious events. He hated British society, believing that England was a land of immoral infidels, and had as little to do with indigenous British culture as possible.

One day my mother asked for an English teacher to give her lessons. When my father came home to find a white woman in his house he was furious. When she left, he screamed at my mother: 'How dare you bring a dirty infidel into my house?' I sat in the next room, listening to the thumps of his fists smashing into her body. The next time he beat her I grabbed onto her to protect her and screamed at him to stop. For a few seconds he stood there, amazed that someone had dared to confront him. Then he started beating me instead. I was 5 years old.

Six months after the first beating, the style of abuse changed horribly. On a day when my father had beaten me I had retreated to my room to escape when the door opened and he stepped into my room with a mixture of loathing and lust on his face. 'You're evil,' he said. 'And you must be punished. But beating isn't enough.' He pulled the blanket away, stripped me naked and sexually abused me. It wasn't long before he started raping me. Every time he did this he would say, 'You are evil, and this is the only way to drive the evil out of you.'

Eventually he got bored with the hurried rapes, or perhaps the bloodied sheets were becoming harder to explain. He started taking me down to the cellar: an empty, cold, rat-infested room where he would lock me for days without food or water and would do whatever he wanted to me. I would lie there, naked, in the cold and damp, dreaming of a make-believe world of lavender and princes in an attempt to forget the hell which my life had become. This abuse went on for years.

When I was 16 I overheard my father talking on the telephone to a relative in Pakistan saying: 'Yes, it's all arranged. We'll be flying out the day after tomorrow, arriving in Karachi that afternoon. Is it all set for the wedding?' They had arranged for me to marry a distant cousin in Pakistan. That night I didn't sleep a wink and the next day when I went to college my heart was pounding. I told my teacher that I was running away from home to avoid an arranged marriage, so she spoke to the deputy head and a social worker arranged for me to stay with a teacher, Mrs Jones. That night I slept in a strange bed, in a strange house, where I felt safe for the first time in years.

The next day the principal called me to his office where I was shocked to see my father. He was weeping openly, which was the first time I had seen him display emotion other than anger or hatred. But his tears were not of sadness for me but anger at the shame he had suffered as a result of my leaving home: 'How will I hold my head up in the community again after the shame you've brought on our family?' I told him I wasn't coming home, then I walked out.

One Sunday the Jones family told me they were going to church and that I should make myself at home. On an impulse I asked if I could go with them. They reluctantly agreed, knowing what a major step this was for a Muslim. The service was wonderful, with a real sense of joy and peace. The minister talked about the life of Jesus and seemed genuinely excited by his faith. I had never enjoyed being in a place of worship before. The Christians there had a concern for the whole world, regardless of whether it was Christian or not. I was discovering a different England; an England of honest, tolerant people whose faith lifted them up and gave meaning to their lives. Not all English people spent their lives getting drunk and sleeping around, as my father had told me.

Soon it was Christmas and the minister talked about God becoming a man who was humble and loving. I leaned over to Julie, my teacher's daughter, and said, 'How does someone become a Christian?' She replied, 'Easy! You just ask Jesus to come into your life. Ask him to forgive your wrongs and give thanks that he died on the cross and rose again for you.' That night I kept thinking about what I had heard. I prayed, 'God, if you are real, if you exist and are a loving God, then I want to know you and I want you to come into my life.' That was the moment I converted. I started reading the Bible and embraced this new-found freedom to be myself, and most of all to be loved. It was not about being worthy; it was about knowing that the love of God was there for me, in spite of everything. For the first time in my life I felt truly at peace.

A couple of years later I decided to be baptized to celebrate and reaffirm my conversion. I decided to invite my family, which I knew was risky; perhaps even naive. At this stage I had never heard of the Islamic teaching of 'apostasy' – that anyone who leaves Islam should be killed. I rang up the brother I had always been closest to and told him what I had in mind. He slammed the phone down. A few days later I was alone in my house studying when I heard a commotion outside. I ran to the window and saw a mob of around forty Pakistani men armed with hammers, sticks and knives. My Dad was at the front with a face masked with fury screaming with the rest of them: 'Filthy traitor! Betrayer of your family! Betrayer of your faith! We're going to rip out your throat! We'll burn you alive!' I was terrified. If Dad broke down the door I knew I would be beaten to death by the mob.

Eventually they went away so I called a friend, packed my things, and left. I went ahead with my baptism but changed the venue as my family knew where it was. From that moment my life changed: I was in hiding and on the run from my own family. I moved house every few months, staying with friends, families of friends, or in temporary rooms. I changed my name, but even with these precautions my father was still trying to hunt me down. He handed out my photo at the mosque with a number to call if anyone saw me. Eventually I moved to the south of England to get out of my father's reach.

My story ends happily because I met a wonderful man and we were married in 2008. I now work with women who have been through similar situations. This issue is on the government's agenda but there is much work to be done to help women who suffer in this way. I frequently speak on the subject in the media and at conferences. I am happy that my story can help to improve the situation for Muslim women. I cannot be silent about injustice. The philosopher Sophocles once said: 'One word frees us of all the

weight and pain of life: that word is love.' This is what
I believe.

Hannah Shah, The Imam's Daughter
(London: Rider Books, 2009)
Adapted and used with permission.

7

Shame in East and West

Shame is not washed, except by blood. *('La yughsal al 'aar,
illa bi-dam')*

Arabic proverb

Most Muslim societies are characterized by an aversion
to shame. This is why Hannah Shah's experience in the
previous Interlude is – sadly – not untypical of the problems faced by some followers of Jesus from Muslim
families who suffer abuse at the hands of relatives
and/or the community who attempt to restore their
'honour'. Hannah's family repeatedly tried to rid themselves of the 'shame' they felt Hannah had brought on
them by her conversion to Christ and subsequent
departure from the family home while still a single
woman. Make no mistake about it: if they could, some
would have killed Hannah in the belief that it is the
only way to regain their lost 'honour' in the belief that
as 'shame' decreases, 'honour' automatically increases,
like a sliding scale.

The compulsion to inflict 'honour punishment' cannot
be categorized as a tenet of Islam but it is a diseased aspect
of some eastern cultures, which can be traced back long
before Islam but which Islam has neither challenged nor

changed. This instinct to punish the one who steals one's 'honour' can also be seen as a perversion of the biblical principle of atonement by blood sacrifice: 'the law requires that nearly everything be cleansed with blood, and without the shedding of blood there is no forgiveness' (Heb. 9:22). This is a biblical rendering of the sentiment expressed by the Arabic proverb at the top of this chapter, where only the shedding of blood can right a wrong.

The restoring of 'honour' is an important underlying motive behind Islamic violence such as 9/11 where Al-Qaeda set out to reclaim the 'honour' of Muslims which they believed had been shamed by the West. Underlying such violence is the belief of many Muslims that 'guilt' – in the western sense – is merely a debt to be paid by a prison sentence or a fine, while 'shame' – in the eastern sense – is seen as an indelible stain that can only be removed by blood, which is able to transfer the 'shame' back onto the culprit.

Having said this, it is not the 'honour/shame' code *per se* that is wrong; in fact the Bible seems to affirm the naming and shaming of offending individuals when it calls for the excommunicating of certain people from the group (Deut. 17:7; 19:19; 21:21; 24:7; 1 Cor. 5:1–12). So, rather than contradicting the honour/shame system, the Bible addresses people who live within it, challenging the unrighteous, inconsistent, unfair and petty basis upon which a community chooses to award 'honour' or assign 'shame'. The Bible also challenges people who operate double standards by assigning 'honour' on the outside while concealing 'shame' on the inside; or people who act immorally in order to gain – or regain – their 'honour'. It is this sort of hypocrisy that Jesus confronted head on.

The more devout a Muslim is, the more their lives are likely to be affected by the pursuit of 'honour' and the avoidance of 'shame'. Take for instance a young Muslim man from Bradford who was employed to deliver bicycles for a leading manufacturer. When his employer discovered that for some months he had been pilfering the occasional bike, the South Asian man was confronted with the evidence. At first he tried to deny the obvious but when he was eventually sacked he went berserk, accusing the management of racism and 'islamophobia'. The following Friday, the young man went confidently to mosque with his prayer cap on as though nothing had happened. On the way there, a dog licked him in front of other Muslims. He was so distressed at having been licked by a dog that he went back home to have a ritual bath and pray for forgiveness. The shame of being licked by an 'unclean' animal was far greater for that young Muslim than his guilt over stealing. This illustrates well the different codes by which Muslims and westerners live.

How Shame Works in the East

The honour/shame code is found throughout the eastern world and was the subject of a recent TV documentary, which featured the largest religious gathering in the world. This was not the Islamic pilgrimage of *hajj*, which attracts up to 4 million Muslims a year to Mecca; it was the Hindu festival of *Kumbh Mela* which is celebrated in rotation around various cities of India, roughly every four years. *Kumbh Mela* attracts up to 60 million pilgrims who bathe on the banks of the holy rivers. A dispute started when restrictions were imposed on bathing rights due to health and hygiene fears about effluent levels. As a result, tens of thousands of naked Sadhus and holy men who bathed there felt that the rivers – and they themselves – were being dishonoured. So they threatened to commit mass suicide by drowning themselves in the disputed holy waters.

This incident shows how, in the East, the honour/shame code can quickly develop beyond the sphere of the personal, the family, the extended family or the community, to become a national or even international political issue. We will therefore look in more detail at how the honour/shame code operates and why it impacts the lives of ordinary Muslims so profoundly. As we do this, it is important to remember that the honour/shame code is no better or worse than other cultures – it is just different.

Here are some pointers that can help us:

1. The concept of 'honour' (*sharaf* or *izzât* in Arabic) and its absence, 'shame' ('*aa*r or *najâf*) are strong themes in most Muslim cultures. Synonyms for the word 'shame' include words such as 'disgrace' ('*ayb*) or 'forbidden' (*harâm*).[1] In cultures under the honour code, the individual is placed on the honour/shame continuum by use of criteria such as family lineage, religious piety, running of a moral household, educational achievement, professional qualification, wealth, or even heroic deeds.

2. 'Honour' is a form of social currency, which is sought after. Such societies are regulated more by the desire for good public standing than by civil law. 'Honour' gives the individual a sense of 'standing', 'face' and 'validity' as a member of the community. Some British Muslims prefer to go to their community elders for a ruling from *shari'a* law on some issues because, if vindicated, they regain a sense of honour in the community at a deeper level than civil law can give them.

3. In a shame-orientated society, social interaction can take the form of symbolic gestures against an opponent, such as yelling, slapping their face, spitting at them or using a shoe to hit them. This was the case in TV images at the end of the second Gulf War when civilians took off their shoes – unclean objects – to beat the fallen statue of President Saddam Hussein. This happened again when the Iraqi journalist Muntadhar al-Zaidi famously threw his shoes at President George Bush in a Baghdad press conference. This behaviour also indicates that the targeted person is lower in status than one's self.

4. 'Shame' can be assigned when an individual allows something to happen to them, as in the case of the young Muslim in Bradford. This is a contrast with the western understanding that you can only be held responsible for something you have intentionally done. This is why the concept of 'man slayer' (i.e. unintentional killing) was provided for in the Mosaic law, along with the cities of refuge which were set up to provide sanctuary from the penalty of the law for premeditated murder (Num. 35:22–28). This is part of the Judeo-Christian heritage in Britain where, to this day, we recognize accidental killing as 'manslaughter' rather than murder. So when the Bradford Muslim was seen being licked by a dog, which is unclean in most eastern cultures, he became 'ritually defiled', which is why he was so traumatized.

5. The only way to escape 'shame' is either to hide the matter, as Joseph did with Mary (Matt. 1:19); or to deny the matter altogether, as Abraham's wife Sarah did when she laughed and denied that she had committed a misdemeanour (Gen. 18:10–15); or to transfer the blame to someone else, as when Adam blamed Eve (Gen. 3:12). As a last resort, 'shame' can be avoided by

moving community. An Arabic proverb says: 'Where you are not known, do whatever you like.' This helps explain why some Arab students I have known (both Muslim and nominal Christian) can be morally loose when they come to the West for study.

6. To illustrate the power of the honour code, the apocryphal story is told in the Middle East of a high-ranking *sheikh* who fell asleep under a palm tree. A poor man passed by and stole his expensive cloak. The *sheikh* was angry and sent his servants to hunt down the thief. When they found him he was put on trial and asked for an explanation. The accused man said, 'Yes, I stole this cloak. I found the *sheikh* sleeping so I had sex with him while he slept, and then took his coat.' The *sheikh* immediately replied, 'There is some mistake. That is not my coat.'

This sort of denial happens because when a person's 'honour' is lost, 'shame' is automatically assigned. The instinct is to simply deny that anything has happened; this includes what an individual does, what they are accused of doing, what inadvertently happens to them (i.e. possible negligence), and what they may fail to do. All this is so important because as 'honour' increases, 'shame' decreases. It is therefore crucial for us to realize that the 'honour/shame code' can threaten the individual's very identity; this is why honour must be maintained at any cost.

7. 'Shame' is applied on the basis of what is known by others about an individual's behaviour. Because the Bible was written in a shame-orientated culture, it recognizes that 'shame' can only be assigned to a thief when he or she is caught (Jer. 2:26). An Afghan proverb says: 'A concealed shame is two thirds forgiven.' So in such cultures it is possible to conceal 'shame' within the privacy of one's heart, but it gets

increasingly harder if the nuclear or extended family know; and the effects of 'shame' cannot be stopped if the misdemeanour becomes publicly known in the wider community.

8. The only way to diminish the damage done by 'shame' is for the individual to take action in order to retain their 'honour'. This can take the form of either shifting the blame to someone else or externalizing it in an 'honour punishment' meted out on the offender. Joseph, the fiancé of Mary the mother of Jesus, demonstrated real character by going against his instinct to protect himself when he discovered that Mary was pregnant before their marriage (Matt. 1:19). When 'honour' is stolen from an individual, they remain 'shamed' if they cannot seize back their 'honour' by 'shaming' the offender in return. This is illustrated when a suicide bomber strikes; for example, the assassin of Benazir Bhutto in Pakistan in 2007. This man took away any possibility of having 'honour' retrieved, by killing himself. In this way, suicide bombers take their self-conferred 'honour' to the grave with them, where it cannot be re-taken by their opponent.

9. In shame-orientated societies, truth-telling can become subservient to 'honour', which means that 'truth' may be withheld in order to protect someone else's 'honour', or to avoid one's own 'shame'. For example, one Muslim asked his western friend to say things which were not true in order to help him. His aim was to get out of one lie by telling a bigger lie to cover up the first. When the western Christian refused to join in, he received one last phone call to say that he had broken the relationship and so it was 'goodbye'.[2] Many westerners will see such behaviour as institutionalized lying. In shame-orientated societies, a lie is

neither right nor wrong; the issue is whether what is being said is 'honourable' or not. In the minds of people living under the honour code, telling an untruth is 'honourable' if the aim is to protect someone's 'honour'; it becomes wrong when the lie is told for selfish ends. This is how people under the honour code are likely to read Bible passages such as Jesus' parable of the two sons in Matthew 21:28–30 who were instructed by their father to go and undertake a task. One son said 'Yes' while he had no intention of doing so – in order to preserve his father's 'honour' – while the other son said 'No', a dishonourable thing to say, but then he went, which was the honourable thing to do.

10. Shame-orientated societies are also group-orientated cultures where it is shameful to be individualistic; for instance, when someone wants to marry for love or wants to leave Islam for Christianity – both of which may shame the entire family.[3] This was the social obligation that was felt by the young Bradford Muslim who pilfered bikes. He was sharing his access to resources with his extended family, which becomes an altruistic form of theft because he was not stealing for himself. This reminds me of a time I was asked to explain to staff in a British Bible college why a non-western Christian student appeared to be helping himself to the property of other students. In the mind of the student, he was merely 'borrowing' things in the same way he would back home, where things operated on a 'what's-yours-is-mine' basis. He had no sense of wrong-doing and he certainly felt no guilt, until it was pointed out to him that the British rules do not operate in the same way. This outlook is typical in cultures which place a higher value on kinship ties, which is a system that is referred to by some anthropologists as 'familism'.[4]

11. So-called 'honour punishments' are the mechanism
    for regaining honour. This has been brought to pub-
    lic attention by authors such as Jasvinder Sanghera, a
    lady from a Sikh background who refused an
    arranged marriage in order to marry for love.[5] She is
    a Sikh counterpart to Hannah Shah, whose story has
    already been told.[6]

    In the past decade, 117 Asian women have disap-
    peared in West Yorkshire alone. One of them was a
    young woman who was presumed murdered simply
    because a romantic song was dedicated to her on a
    local Asian radio station.[7] I was moved to see
    Jasvinder Sanghera presented with an award from
    the Asian actress Meera Syal for her work in helping
    Asian women who have been abused by honour
    punishments. As the award was handed over, Ms
    Syal commented pointedly on how honour had been
    restored to that community.[8] I wonder how many
    western viewers understood the deeper message in
    that statement.

12. The fear of 'shame' means that many Muslims strug-
    gle to admit defeat or accept culpability of any sort.
    'Shame' can come from the breaking of social norms
    such as dressing immodestly, failing to show respect
    for one's parents, failing to submit to an arranged
    marriage, or being alone in a house with a member of
    the opposite sex when there is no chaperone around.

13. In Japanese culture, the blame and/or rage that is
    provoked by the 'shame' inflicted by scandal, bank-
    ruptcy or moral failure tends to be internalized. This
    leads to self-harm such as when Japanese people
    commit suicide (*harikiri*) in response to dishonour.
    This is the opposite of *kamikaze* which is when the
    suicide becomes a heroic act of honour. The opposite
    is true in Arabized cultures where the blame and

rage provoked by shame is externalized and honour is regained by revenge, such as the 9/11 attacks on America which were mainly a response to the military, economic and cultural influence of the West in Muslim territories.

14. In the Confucianist culture of Korea, men are expected to be quiet and let women do the talking. This is due to the view that silence – unless one has wise words to say – is preferable to talking. To say little in such cultures is considered dignified and therefore honourable. This too has a scriptural basis: 'Even fools are thought wise if they keep silent, and discerning if they hold their tongues' (Prov. 17:28).

The Western Counterpart of Guilt

The counterpart to the concept of 'shame' in the East is the western counterpart of 'guilt'. In one sense these two words are used by people in eastern and western cultures to refer to the same thing. However, there is a subtle difference which is best understood by seeing 'shame' and 'guilt' as words that are used in two alternative worldviews where they ensure that prescribed social behaviour is adhered to.

For example, parents in 'guilt-orientated' western societies might be heard saying to their children: 'Don't throw that stone, it's wrong', while parents in 'shame-orientated' eastern societies might be heard saying to their children: 'Don't throw that stone, it's *shameful*.'[9] The difference between the words '*wrong*' and 'shameful' is significant because it says a lot about how the two cultures work. Western cultures tend to think in ethical categories of 'right' and 'wrong' rather than 'honour' and 'shame', so when an action is wrong, 'guilt' is assigned to the person who did it. It is interesting to note that even with the influence of secularization, people's God-given conscience still seems to trouble them.

For some western cynics, the notion of 'guilt' is seen – unfairly in my view – as a by-product of Christianity. Take, for example, Sigmund Freud who was part of an intellectual movement committed to the abolition of the external sources of 'guilt', including religiously induced 'guilt'. Another example is Oscar Wilde who famously quipped that the best way to resist temptation is to give in to it.

A recent campaign by the British Secular Humanist Society sponsored posters on buses that said: 'There probably isn't a God, so relax and enjoy life!' This perceived link between religion and drudgery seems to be part of an atheistic outlook.

By contrast, shame-orientated societies have a more corporate worldview than is the case in the West. This means that it is 'shame' rather than rules which determines people's behaviour. However, this is not to suggest that Muslim people do not have a conscience – far from it. Many Muslims have spoken to me about their troubled conscience. I have found the Arabic proverb to be true, which says: 'A lone hermit in the desert may feel *guilt* but he cannot feel *shame*.'[10] So while Muslims feel 'shame' publicly and feel 'guilt' inwardly, westerners might feel 'guilt' publicly but feel 'shame' inwardly.

Shame in the West

It is important to remember that eastern and western cultures have both 'shame' and 'guilt' in them; it is just that 'shame' is more dominant in the East and 'guilt' is more dominant in the West. So 'shame' does exist in the West but it has less social control, partly because the West is a more secularized society that has relegated its Judeo-Christian values to the margins of its value system and is therefore able to take contrasting views about what constitutes 'shameful behaviour' in its stride. For example, in 2008 Max Mosley, a wealthy and influential public figure in the UK, was exposed by the press, with photo, evidence, as having indulged in exotic sexual misdemeanours with prostitutes in a Nazi-themed party. Rather than being shamed by the revelation, Mosley sued the newspapers for 'invasion of privacy' and defamation of character for being accused of being a Nazi sympathizer based on the fact that he spoke in German during the alleged orgies. Clearly the western psyche operates very differently to easterners in these issues. This is partly due to the fact that even people who commit public fraud or act immorally are punished for only a short while, with the exception of paedophiles who remain in a more serious category.

The Oxford Dictionary defines 'shame' as the 'feeling of humiliation caused by the consciousness of guilt or folly . . . disgrace, discredit or intense regret . . . the imposing of constraint on behaviour due to disgrace'. This definition of 'shame' is limited for two reasons: firstly, because it is only a 'western' definition; and secondly, because it might well be challenged in post-modern Britain where people tend to disagree among themselves about what 'shame' might be in a society that is not convinced that it needs a 'moral compass'.

As a result of changing moral values in western countries such as Britain, there can be different *kinds* as well as different *degrees* of 'shame'. Western researchers tend to define 'shame' in two broad categories, including 'good shame' and 'bad shame'.[11] 'Good shame' is what happens *to* the individual, such as when a woman is raped (i.e. shame as violation), or when someone is always put down (i.e. shame by low self-esteem) or, in a lesser sense, when a lecturer finds his trouser zip undone during a keynote talk (i.e. shame as embarrassment). 'Bad shame' is what is committed *by* the individual, such as when an executive director of a company is exposed for fraud (i.e. shame as humiliation), or when a marine receives a dishonourable discharge (i.e. shame as failure), or when a devout Catholic woman kills her illegitimate newborn (i.e. shame as being looked down on and judged).[12]

Having said all this, both 'good' and 'bad' forms of shame tend to be assigned differently in eastern cultures. For example, becoming a rape victim in the West may be assigned to the category of 'good shame'; in the East, however, it is seen as 'bad shame' but for different reasons – namely that it leads to the loss of marriageable status (i.e. shame by low-ranking).

However, Britain has not always been such a guilt-orientated culture. As far back as William Shakespeare, 'shame' was a common word which was mentioned much more than 'guilt'. Take, for instance, the line in Shakespeare's play *Tamburlaine the Great*: 'Mine *honour* is my life; both grow in one; take *honour* from me and my life is done' (italics mine).[13] This suggests that in the Bard's England, the emphasis on 'shame' was much closer to what is found in the East today. Some observers say that Britain is returning to a greater sense of community, and with it, the beginnings of a renewed awareness of 'shame'. This is thought to be due to dissatisfaction with individualism, which has led to isolation and meaninglessness.

We have seen that it is a matter of courtesy to convey the gospel to a Muslim in ways that they can understand

and relate to. We now also know that an important felt-need of Muslims is to find a solution to their sense of hidden 'guilt' and their fear of public 'shame'. We turn next to examine how the gospel applies to a person with a shame-orientated mindset. We will also identify the characteristics of the eastern telling of the gospel and begin to unpack how this differs from what we are familiar with.

An eastern telling of the gospel – helpful hint No. 4

Bystanders at Jesus' crucifixion hurled insults including: 'He trusts in God. Let God rescue him now if he wants him' (Matt. 27:43–44). This perfectly articulates the Middle Eastern (and Islamic) assumption that anyone who is a king with authority would assert himself with pride and forcefulness. He would never passively accept weakness and vulnerability. But this is precisely what Jesus did on the cross where he embraced the opposite of the Islamic ideal of strength and power. Jesus' death demonstrated the fact that God can do as he pleases – including the choice to enter the lower echelons of society and willingly accept a shameful death in order to deliver us from 'shame'.

Muslims can be helped to understand why the shame of the cross was necessary to redeem us. To do this we need to explain the cross in ways they can relate to; for example, that on the cross Jesus became the 'Black Stone' of God. This is a reference to the corner of the meteorite stone that forms the base of the *ka'aba* – the draped cube-like structure at the Grand Mosque in Mecca. The *ka'aba* has become the focus of the *hajj* pilgrimage and, as such, is the geographical and spiritual epicentre of Islam. Muslim legend has it that, when a Muslim kisses the Black Stone, their sins are transferred to it – which is why it has turned black.

In the same way, on the cross Jesus absorbed our sin, guilt and shame. Psalm 2 invites us to 'Kiss his [God's] son . . . blessed are all who take refuge in him' (Ps. 2:12). Also, in the language of the Bible, Jesus' wounds 'heal us' (i.e. make us whole; Isa. 53:5b) when he carried our sorrows and laid the iniquity of us all on him (Isa. 53:6b). The predominant western view understands this in terms of penal substitution (i.e. 'Jesus died *instead of* us'), while the eastern view understands it more readily as intercession (i.e. Jesus died *between* God and us, as the go-between who brings God and us back into right relationship).

Notes

1. Jabbour, Nabil, *Unshackled and Growing – Muslims and Christians on the Road to Freedom* (Colorado Springs: Dawson Media, 2006), p. 83.
2. Blincoe, Bob, *Faces of Islam – Honor and Shame: an Open Letter to Evangelical Leaders*, in *Mission Frontiers*, December 2001 (Pasadena: USCWM), p. 20.
3. UNICEF Report.
4. Patai, Raphael, *The Arab Mind* (New York: Scribner's & Sons, 1976), p. 94.
5. Sanghera, Jasvinder, *Shame* (London: Hodder & Stoughton), 2007.
6. Shah, Hannah, *The Imam's Daughter* (London: Rider Books, 2009).
7. Wilkes, David, *Daily Mail*, Thursday 18 June 2009, p. 9.
8. *The Pride of Britain Awards* 2009, ITV1, 7 October 2009.

9 Patai, Raphael, *The Arab Mind* (New York: Scribner's & Sons, 1976), p. 94.

10 Ausubel, David P., *The Relationship between Shame and Guilt in the Socializing Process*, in *Psychological Review* Vol. 2, No. 5, September 1955, pp. 379, 382, 389.

11 McIlroy, David, *Honour and Shame – Towards a Biblical Mind*, Cambridge Papers Vol. 14 No. 2, p. 1.

12 Wilkes, David, *Daily Mail*, Thursday 18 June 2009, p. 9.

13 Shakespeare, William, *Tamburlaine the Great*, Part I, Act IV Scene IV.

8.

The Gospel and Shame-based Societies

> Muslim people need to know that to embrace the gospel is not the cause of their shame but the solution to it.
>
> *Roland Muller*

Imagine the gospel to be like a painting that is to be shown to a worldwide audience, all of whom are colour-blind. The westerners cannot see blues (i.e. 'honour') and greens (i.e. 'shame'), while the eastern audience cannot see reds (i.e. 'sin') and yellows (i.e. 'guilt'). This colour-blindness causes people from both cultural outlooks to have difficulty seeing everything that has been lovingly put into the painting – that is, not without help from each other. This predicament exists because people from both cultural world-views only look for what they expect to find. This is what is going on when westerners fail to see 'shame' in the Bible while being more sensitive to the Bible's references to 'guilt'.

The Western Telling of the Gospel

We saw in Chapter 1 how western evangelicalism is rooted in the Protestant theology of the Reformers. These were Europeans whose biographies show that many of them were trained lawyers as well as theologians; among the better known names are Martin Luther, John Calvin, Ulrich Zwingli and Hugo Grotius. These men were therefore naturally drawn to the Bible's legal and forensic metaphors, which describe the human predicament using the language of the courtroom: humankind is guilty in the dock; the sentence has been passed and we now owe a debt we cannot pay; Jesus intervened to pay the debt he did not owe by taking the punishment instead of us, so we can be acquitted. It is therefore not surprising that the 'penal substitution' model of the atonement has become the most prominent in the West, where it resonates well with our Greco-Roman concept of 'justice'.

Following the Reformation, the era of European 'enlightenment' made us an increasingly scientific society where only things that are quantifiable were seen as important. 'Guilt' could be quantified because a bad action could be analyzed and appropriate punishment could be assigned to fit the crime. However, 'shame' cannot be so easily quantified, which may have contributed to a lack of interest in it in the West. This is another example of how theology develops within a cultural context.

As a result of the European cultural context, the starting point for the telling of the gospel in western evangelical theology has become 'original sin' which we have all carried like a cancer of the soul, from our mother's womb (Rom. 5:12–21). This has given rise to presenting the gospel through the easy to understand format of the 'four spiritual laws':

1. We need to be saved (Rom. 3:23; 6:23; Isa. 53:6; Heb. 9:27; John 3:3, 6).
2. We cannot save ourselves (Prov. 14:12; Gal. 2:16; Eph. 2:8–9; John 14:6).
3. God saves us by Jesus' death and resurrection (John 3:16; Rom. 6:23; 1 Thess. 5:9–10; 1 Pet. 3:18).
4. Jesus has the power to both save us and keep us (Heb. 7:25; Jude 24; Heb. 2:18; 2 Cor. 5:17).[1]

Although this format has become popular around the world – due to western Christian influence – we must recognize that it reflects the western preference for logical progression; in this case, from human need (i.e. the problem), to God's action (i.e. the solution), to our response (i.e. the application).

Paul, the Theological Bridge between East and West

The problem is that people with an eastern mindset do not think in such a linear way. This is why God's choice of Saul of Tarsus as a cross-cultural ambassador of the gospel was so strategic. He was a 'chosen instrument' for the communication of the gospel to 'the Gentiles . . . and to the people of Israel' (Acts 9:15). He was an ultra-Orthodox Jew from the Gentile town of Tarsus in Asia Minor. His birth name – 'Saul' – was the Hebrew (i.e. eastern) name from which, after his conversion, the Roman (i.e. western) equivalent of 'Paul' was adopted.

These two names reflect Paul's dual heritage, which gave him access to both eastern and western thought patterns. It is this that sensitised him to the fact that 'Jews demand signs and Greeks look for wisdom' (1 Cor. 1:22). Paul was culturally equipped to contextualize the gospel for the multi-cultural churches of Greece, Italy and Asia, where Jews and Gentiles worshipped together from Europe, Asia and North Africa. This dual heritage also enabled Paul to understand the gospel from within the Semitic or eastern outlook – which Muslims are more at home with – and 'translate' it into the Greco-Roman outlook, which is accessible to westerners.

Paul showed how Jesus' physical death enabled those who trust in him to be 'reconciled' to God. It was this reconciliation that made us 'free from accusation' (i.e. a solution to 'guilt') and also free from 'blemish' (i.e. a solution to defilement, which is an aspect of 'shame'; Col. 1:22). In this way, Paul's use of the word 'justification' and the legal language of the Roman courtroom would have greater resonance with Europeans – and was taken up by the Reformers – whereas Tom Wright also points to the broader emphasis of Paul that is painted in colours less familiar:

> God must 'judge' the world in the sense of 'putting it right' and God has brought this judgement into the middle of history in the covenant-fulfilling work of Jesus Christ, dealing with sin through his death, launching the new world in his resurrection and sending his Spirit to enable human beings, through repentance and faith, to become . . . advance parts of that new creation.[2]

So as well as the legal language of 'justification', Paul also used the language of 'righteousness', which resonated with Jews, for whom 'shame' and 'defilement' before the law, were a live issue. An example of this was his choice of words in his letter to the multi-cultural church in Rome, where he encouraged both Jews and Gentiles to relate to Abraham as the first to achieve the status of 'justified' or 'righteous' before God. He did so *before* he was circumcised (Rom. 4:9–11). As such, Abraham is the model of 'righteousness' with God by faith (Rom. 4:16b–17).

Paul's use of the word 'righteousness' (Rom. 1:16, 17) was rooted in the Hebrew concept of *tsedaqah* or right-standing with God within the context of his covenant with Israel. This found its fulfilment in the work of Christ on the cross whereby the believer can be seen by God as having fulfilled all the requirements of the law and so be declared 'righteous'. The point here is that faith without religious performance is rewarded by God; a point that was also endorsed by Moses who was the ultimate champion of Jewish religious law (Rom. 3:21). The good news for Muslims is therefore that God's righteousness can be obtained via this new arrangement (i.e. covenant), which is available to the circumcised and uncircumcised alike. All must come to God by the same route of 'faith' (Rom. 3:30).

However, as church history unfolded, theological tensions emerged in the church in eastern and western cultures – namely the church of the Eastern Roman Empire (the Byzantium Orthodox Church) and the western Roman Church (the Roman Catholic Church). The 'guilt/shame' tension was just one such issue which caused a theological separation in spite of the fact that both sides were influenced, to differing degrees, by Greco-Roman heritage.

Since the theological separation, the Eastern Orthodox Churches have engaged more naturally with issues such as 'mystery' as seen in the Trinity, the relationship between the human and divine aspects of Jesus, our relationship to the saints that have gone before us, the interface between the natural and supernatural realms, the activity of angelic and demonic beings in the world, and

God's miraculous power made available through 'anointed' people, objects and places, in order to heal and deliver from the demonic.[3] Themes such as these resonate not only with eastern Christians, but also increasingly with followers of Jesus from a Muslim background, some of whom are choosing to attach themselves to Orthodox churches where, in spite of the use of icons and the historic reticence to relate to Muslims, they are beginning to be more accepted and are being baptized.

In contrast, the church in the West, particularly after the Protestant Reformation and the Enlightenment, has developed a more systematic, rationalist and individualist approach to theology. It is less comfortable with 'mystery' or the supernatural realm. Martin Goldsmith describes how, as a new mission worker, he began to encounter the supernatural in the Muslim world, which posed questions which had not been addressed in his mission preparation, and which led to a paradigm shift:

> Experience of the demonic work of evil spirits came as a shock to me when I first went to work in Asia. Having come to Christ and grown in my Christian life within the context of conservative evangelical teaching, I had never witnessed such activity of Satan. And in my biblical and theological studies, it would have been quite unacceptable to talk or write about demons or evil spirits, although the gospels frequently refer to them.[4]

This de-emphasizing of the supernatural seems to be linked to the fact that, during the Reformation, the reforming theologians focused on resisting the excesses of Roman Catholic dogma, relics and the superstitious paraphernalia at shrines. In doing this, theological changes occurred, including issues such as a de-emphasis on the power and demonstration of the Holy Spirit – a vital aspect of the gospel. Muslims, like the ancient Jews, are impacted by 'supernatural signs' (1 Cor. 1:22), as I discovered when Pentecostal pastors in the Middle East would tell me how Muslims occasionally bring their sick and demonised to Christians for prayer in Jesus' name. If only more western Christians would make it known to Muslims that they are willing to pray for the sick and even interpret dreams which God uses to speak to them.

However, it seems to me that the western de-emphasis of the supernatural is due – in part – to the fact that, while breaking with the teaching of the Roman Catholic Church, the European Reformers lost touch with the heritage of the five branches of the Orthodox Church: Greek, Russian, Ethiopian, Armenian and Coptic. Western evangelicalism is the poorer for its apparent reluctance to recognize the theology of these non-western Christian traditions.

During the theological divergence of eastern and western theology, there were also some notable eastern dissenters, such as John Chrysostom (c. AD 347). So eloquent was Chrysostom's preaching, he was nicknamed 'the golden mouthed'. In prophetic fashion, he majored on issues that others minored on; for example, he challenged those who used their position in the church for personal material benefit. It is worth noting that according to tradition, none of Chrysostom's 680 written sermons were about 'justification by faith' from the western perspective of the 'legal/penal' model of the atonement. This is likely because Chrysostom would have been speaking from a more eastern point of view which, while affirming that the doctrine of 'justification by faith' is a seminal part of the gospel, would nevertheless define 'saving faith' as being what Abraham exercised. This was not a one-off act but a lifelong process of trusting obedience to God, so when the Bible says, 'Abraham believed the LORD and it was credited to him as righteousness' (Gen. 15:6), Chrysostom understood it to be a summary of Abraham's life. This was also the sense in which the apostle Paul used the term when he defined his ministry as the calling of all nations to the 'obedience of faith' (Rom. 1:5).

This contrasts sharply with the more extreme forms of western evangelicalism, which talk about 'saving faith' as though it were a currency with which to enter into a transaction with God who is portrayed as a divine vending machine, into which the coin of faith is inserted in order to extract whatever we may need. This is unhelpful to people from a Muslim background because their eastern understanding of a lifestyle of submission to God is part of their perception of what faith is. To communicate faith in the way Abraham did enables a Muslim to understand faith in Christ in the broader biblical sense rather than the 'accept-believe-confess' rendering of the gospel – which is not found in the words of Jesus; although it can be found in the epistles.[5]

The Intercessory View of the Atonement

So the gospel for Muslims must emphasize an eastern view of the atonement. The models of the atonement that are espoused in the West include the following, which are a human attempt to make the fullest sense of Jesus' final declaration from the cross: 'It is finished!' They suggest that at that moment:

- Satan's *tyranny ended* and the captives were set free (i.e. the liberation model)

- the just *consequences of sin* had been met (i.e. the legal model)
- the *penalty* for sin had been paid (i.e. the penal model)
- the *debt* had been paid in full (i.e. the economic model)
- the ultimate *sacrifice* had been made (i.e. the sacrificial model)
- the stain of sin was *cleansed* (i.e. the purification model)
- the *new covenant* in Jesus' blood was established (i.e. the covenantal model)
- God had *won* the battle with evil (i.e. the 'Christus Victor' or triumphal model)
- God was *satisfied* that everything had been done in accordance with his character (i.e. the transactional model).[6]

Clearly all the historically accepted models of the atonement are true and biblical. However, whether eastern or western in emphasis, they are all facets of a much greater whole. James Atkinson captures this beautifully: 'The truth lies less in one theory, perhaps not even in their sum, but rather in the illuminating cross-light they shed on a profound mystery.'[7] Award-winning Croatian theologian Miroslav Volf offers the following profound insight into the mystery of the atonement; one in which each member of humanity is invited into the fellowship of the Trinity:

When God sets out to embrace the enemy, the result is the cross. On the cross the dancing circle of self-giving and mutually indwelling divine persons opens up for the enemy; in the agony of the passion, the movement stops for a brief moment and a fissure appears so that sinful humanity can join in (see John 17:21). We, the enemies, are embraced by the divine persons who love us with the same love with which they love each other and therefore make space for us within their own eternal embrace.[8]

The 'legal' and 'penal' models of the atonement stress what Christ has done on our behalf and the *positional* benefits for the believer. This language serves the needs of people in individualistic cultures.

On the other hand in eastern cultures, which have not been exposed to the western emphasis, the stress tends to be on what Christ has done *with* us at the cross. By that I mean to say that Jesus took humanity with himself into the experience of death, burial, resurrection and ascension. The impact is less on the individual believer as the corporate body and it gravitates towards the *relational* benefit. This is a corporate and mystical understanding of the cross. It is present in the apostles' doctrine; for example, eastern theology tends to emphasize the fact that the believer in Jesus is united *relationally* with Christ in his death and resurrection life (Rom. 6:1–11). So when Jesus died, the debt of humankind (i.e. 'guilt/shame') died with him. This understanding fits the eastern psyche which says 'I am because we are'. In eastern societies people are 'in it together' – which is reflected in the practice of a more corporate devotional life in the eastern churches.

By contrast, the western concept of 'me, my quiet time, and my walk with God' is rooted in a western mindset which is reflected in our spirituality. When the Bible uses the word 'advocate' (1 John 2:1) it is another legal term which originated in the Greco-Roman courtroom. This word is used today of barristers who speak up on behalf of the accused. A term that resonates better with

Muslims is the word 'intercessor'. This is a more 'relational' term, which describes the eastern social function whereby a friend 'stands in the gap' between two conflicting parties. In the Old Testament, Job referred to this function when he said 'if only there were someone to arbitrate between us [God and himself], to lay a hand on us both' (Job 9:33). In some Muslim societies, someone in this social role is called a *wasta* (i.e. a go-between or middle-man). The role that is played by the *wasta* is varied; it can be as a source of information and reassurance, which was the case when I was asked to perform the function in Egypt by a Coptic Orthodox family I knew. They needed to glean information about the suitability of a male work colleague of mine who they were considering as a potential marriage partner for a female relative of theirs. Another role of a *wasta* is as an 'arbitrator' who pleads the cause of someone else with a view to achieving their vindication – another honour/shame concept (see also Job 27:6; 29:14).

Jesus is also described as the 'mediator' between God and humankind, which is another form of intercession. He will continue this intercessory role until the end of time (1 Tim. 2:5). On the cross, Jesus 'made *intercession* for the transgressors' (Isa. 53:12c), which made the cross an intercessory act (Eph. 5:2; Heb. 9:26; 10:11–14). Since the cross Jesus has been in heaven, standing in the gap: he 'always lives to intercede' for us (Heb. 7:25). So the 'intercessory' view of the atonement is an equally valid way of understanding the cross.

Jesus' Power over Defilement

In shame-orientated societies, 'shame' can also come from 'ritual defilement'. This occurs through things such as eating non-*halal* food products, menstruation, the emission of semen, touching the dead, breaking bodily prohibitions such as using the right hand rather than the left to toilet oneself, or from medical conditions such as 'fistula' wounds incurred during childbirth that can make a woman incontinent. 'Defilement' is a taboo that magnifies the effect of 'shame' within the community. This is what impacted the young Bradford Muslim who was unaffected by the guilt incurred by pilfering bikes, yet he became distressed when he was licked by a dog, which is a ritually unclean animal for most Muslims.

> Whereas *guilt* involves distress over what a person has done, *shame* may involve the questioning of who a person is and whether it is legitimate for that person even to exist. *Shame* [and *defilement*] function at a level much deeper than guilt and may motivate suicide [or the honour killing of someone else].[9]

Jesus spoke into the issue of 'defilement' when he warned us not to get lost in the minutiae of religious performance, which he referred to as to 'strain out a gnat but swallow a camel' (Matt. 23:24). He challenged observances such as ceremonial hand washing and *kosher* diet among Jewish leaders and insisted that it is not what goes into the body that defiles so much as what comes out of it, because it is what comes out of our mouth that betrays what is in our heart and makes us ritually impure in God's sight (Matt. 15:10–11, 18, 20).

The Pharisaic attitude to the minutiae of religious law has been carried over into Islam's *shari'a* law. Many Muslims can be as concerned as some orthodox Jews about ceremonial cleanliness and the need to avoid 'defilement'. So the 'eastern telling' of the gospel emphasizes the fact that Jesus demonstrated his authority over 'defilement' by deliberately selecting for healing people whose lives were blighted by 'defilement'; for instance, the woman with a menstrual condition, which caused a discharge of blood for twelve years (Matt. 9:20–22) and the man suffering from leprosy (Matt. 8:3–4). Such miracles were a visual aid to understanding Jesus' power to cleanse people, inside and out (Matt. 8:1–4). By touching the 'unclean', Jesus demonstrates to Muslims his power to make the 'defiled' holy; a significant sign of his divinity. He also challenges the concern of many Muslims that a prophet of Islam – let alone God himself – would touch what was defiled. In order to perform such miracles, Jesus broke the law of Moses by touching the 'unclean', which to onlookers was like inserting a finger into a septic wound and rubbing it into an abrasion on your own face. According to the law of Moses, when he touched the man, Jesus should have become defiled, both in the superstitious sense that leprosy was contagious (which remains unproven), as well as in the ritual sense that he would become 'ceremonially unclean' (Lev. 13:3, 45).

Regardless of the fact that Jesus had broken the *torah*, he was clearly vindicated, because the ceremonially unclean person was made 'clean', which meant that God was pleased with the action. So instead of the 'clean' person becoming 'defiled', divine life expelled defilement so that the 'defiled' person became 'clean'. Jesus then commanded the man to show himself to the priests and offer a sacrifice of thanksgiving in order to fulfil the requirements of the law of Moses for someone who had been cleansed of leprosy (Matt. 8:4). It seems that Jesus was careful to fulfil the law which – as we saw earlier – he gave to Moses, in the first place. The healing of the man with leprosy is a striking illustration of Jesus' divinity being made explicit without him saying a word – a point that was first brought to my attention by a Muslim.

The 'eastern telling' of the gospel draws attention to the fact that 'shame' and 'defilement' influence the behaviour of people throughout the Bible. For example:

- In the creation account, Adam and Eve were naked but 'felt no shame' (Gen. 2:25) – that is, until they rebelled against God, at which point they realized they were naked and covered themselves. They felt 'shame' because they were naked, but not 'guilt' because they had rebelled against God (Gen. 3:10).
- The women of an eastern household are the custodians of its 'honour'. Family honour was snatched away from Jacob's household when his daughter, Dinah, was raped by Shechem, the son of a neighbouring family (Gen. 34). Shechem did not follow the expected social process by getting permission for what should have been a contractual arrangement between the two families. The 'shame' became 'defilement' because of the discharge of semen during the rape. This compounded the family reaction and made it more severe (v. 13). Dinah's brothers spoke 'deceitfully' to Shechem and his family, offering them the option of intermarriage between the two families on the provision that the household of Shechem should be circumcised. They waited until Shechem and his entire family were in painful recovery, before attacking and slaughtering them en masse in an 'honour killing'.
- When the obnoxious man Nabal dishonoured King David, it caused an 'honour/shame' confrontation in which David planned an honour punishment in order to regain his standing, until Abigail intervened as an 'intercessor' to avert bloodshed. David allowed

himself to be talked out of his violent defence of his honour, choosing the greater honour of leaving the retribution to God; an action which God vindicated (1 Sam. 25).

- Public 'shame' was involved if a woman's skirt was lifted (Ezek. 23:26–30). 'Shame' could also be inflicted in war as a punishment by cutting off part of a man's clothing around the waist, revealing his buttocks (1 Sam. 24:4–6; 2 Sam. 10:4–5).

- Communal events, such as engagement parties, weddings and funerals were crucial opportunities for families to showcase their good standing (or otherwise). Professional people were hired to rejoice or wail as appropriate. Both Jesus and Peter had to put such mourners out of the room before raising a person from the dead (Matt. 9:24–5; Acts 9:39–40).

- Jesus was dealing in the currency of 'honour' and 'shame' during his combative encounters with the Jewish religious establishment. When he provoked a synagogue leader to use the letter of the law as a weapon in an open attack on his honour, Jesus rebuffed the criticism by using 'shame' when he called the synagogue leader's role into question by exposing him as a dysfunctional shepherd in Israel. The text says that the onlookers were 'delighted' by the 'honourable' things Jesus said and did (Luke 13:10–17). Jesus personified 'honour' to the extent that when people challenged him, they lost face in a 'challenge and riposte' form of combat.[10]

Ritual cleanliness is still a part of the lives of many ordinary Muslims today. Researcher Bruce Thomas[11] found that for some Muslims to remain ritually clean, they feel the need to observe the following sort of rituals:

- taking care to ensure that you are facing Mecca when you fall asleep (and even when being buried)
- remembering to utter the *bismil* (i.e. saying 'In the name of God the Merciful and the Compassionate') before a significant action, such as an exam
- being particular about using the left hand to toilet oneself
- taking care when blowing the nose, burping, or having flatulence, which must be done in a prescribed way
- avoiding sitting on a seat after a woman, before her body heat has gone
- avoiding the touching of urine, semen, faeces or menstrual discharge
- abstaining from eating pork or drinking alcohol
- avoiding the lick of animals such as dogs.

When Muslim people read the Bible, they are likely to grasp – more easily than westerners do – that Jesus was addressing the issue of 'defilement' as well as 'shame'. The gospel for Muslims is that Jesus is the solution to both. This is the ideal place to arrive at, but how can a Muslim be enabled to engage with the gospel when it asks them to humble their heart and embrace their brokenness before God and ask for his grace? (Prov. 3:34; Jas. 4:6b).

The hurdle that needs to be overcome in order for this to happen, is that the gospel – at least as it is told in the West – has to first become bad news before it can become good news. In other words, the recipient must recognize that there is a problem; we are not morally neutral as Islam teaches, rather we are prisoners of our sinful human nature, which is actively biased against the ways of God. This fact is at the heart of the battle to convey the gospel to anyone, whether they are a Muslim or not.

Many secular westerners reject the idea that they have a sin-problem because they have devised a 'morality of convenience' which they defend on the basis that they are an average law-abiding person and that they try to do good where they can. Easterners too reject the thought of being a 'sinner' because to them a 'sinner' is a criminal or an evil person. For a Muslim to admit to being culpable of 'sin' would mean, to their mind, losing face in the opinion of their community, as well as running the risk of being assigned to eternal damnation by God. A Turkish proverb says: 'Even if shame were made of silk, no one would wear it.' This issue lies at the heart of the Muslim rejection of the gospel, which challenges what I call 'DIY religion' of self-effort by insisting that we need divine help (i.e. grace).

Having seen that the heart of the gospel is the death of Jesus Christ to save us, we now know that there are various ways of understanding this mystery, and western theology is just one aspect of the bigger picture. An eastern view of the atonement is also valid and is more helpful to Muslims because it addresses the 'shame' issue more effectively than the 'substitutionary' model.

In the final chapter we will explore ways of applying the eastern telling of the gospel to a Muslim, for whom 'shame' is a destructive stain on the character which threatens their social standing and very identity. We saw in Chapter 7 how in the Muslim psyche, 'shame' can only be removed by the shedding of blood, which alone can transfer the 'shame' to another. The potential of this belief is clear. When a Muslim engages with the fact that the shedding of Jesus' blood was the divine transfer which cleanses 'shame', as well as 'sin' and 'guilt', they can discover that the cross was the anvil upon which

God – in Christ – beat out justice and mercy and released forgiveness and grace for all, in the most sublime act of 'intercession' in human history.

Notes

[1] *Four Things God Wants You to Know!* (London: Scripture Gift Mission).

[2] Wright, Tom, *Justification: God's Plan and Paul's Vision* (London: SPCK, 2009), p. 223.

[3] Cunningham, Mary, *Faith in the Byzantine World* (Oxford: Lion Publishing, 2002), pp. 123, 141–58.

[4] Goldsmith, Martin, *Beyond Beards and Burqas: Connecting with Muslims* (Leicester: IVP, 2009), p. 70.

[5] Muller, Roland, *Honour and Shame – Unlocking the Door* (New Jersey: Xlibris Corporation, 2000).

[6] Fowler, James, A., *Concepts and Models of the Atonement* (USA: Christ in You Ministries, 1998).
http://www.christinyou.net/pages/atonement.html

[7] Atkinson, James A., *Concepts of the Atonement*, a paper in *A Dictionary of Christian Theology*, ed. Alan Richardson (London: SCM Press Ltd, 1969), p. 24.

[8] Volf, Miroslav, *Exclusion & Embrace: a Theological Exploration of Identity, Otherness and Reconciliation* (Nashville: Abingdon, 1996), p. 129.

[9] Muller, Roland, *Honour and Shame – Unlocking the Door* (New Jersey: Xlibris Corporation, 2000).

[10] Neyrey, Jerome, H., *Honor and Shame in the Gospel of Matthew* (Louisville: Westminster John Knox Press, 1998), pp. 44–5.

[11] Thomas, Bruce, *The Gospel for Shame Cultures: a Paradigm Shift*, in *Evangelical Mission Quarterly* (July 1994).

9.

Gospel for Muslims

'All of us have become like one who is *unclean*, and all our
righteous acts are like filthy rags [i.e. ceremonially defiled].'
Isaiah 64:6

One of my American friends talks about the western tendency to offer a 'pre-packaged' gospel. He is referring to
the logical thought pattern in the West where 'the
gospel' tends to be presented through the life, death and
resurrection of Jesus, and the call to respond to him.
Bishop Tom Wright brings the corrective when he says:
'Western tradition has often failed to recognize that
scripture forms a story whose climax is the coming of
the unique son of God.'[1] This brings us back to the asser-
tion in Chapter 1 that the gospel, particularly for
Muslims, begins in Genesis, not Matthew, and that it
includes the entire flow of the Bible's story of salvation
from 'sin', 'guilt', 'shame' and 'defilement'. The whole
character of God, as revealed throughout the Bible, must
be applied to the total need of the individual. So we
need to 'unpack' what we are used to thinking of in a
'pre-packed' way.

The languages Muslims speak are visual or full of
word pictures. This is because the cultures the languages

serve receive information more readily through mental imagery than through logical argument; this is why Jesus told so many stories (i.e. parables). Likewise, the gospel for Muslims is best told through word pictures. Here is such a picture: The eastern telling of the gospel is like a string of pearls with two colours of pearl on the string. The string itself is the chronological storyline of the Bible and the two colours of pearl are the *incidents* that occurred during the storyline and then the *illustrations* which illuminate the incidents. Tom Wright puts this succinctly:

> The story, of which Jesus Christ is the focal point, is the story of God's whole creation, focused . . . on Abraham and his family and their story as the promise-bearing people; it is also the story, as yet unfinished, of what Jesus Christ continues to do and teach by the gift of his Holy Spirit in advance of the day when what God did for Jesus at Easter he will do, not only for all his people but for the whole creation.[2]

The Qur'an refers to Christians as *ahl i-kitab* ('the People of the Bible'); it is therefore fitting for Muslims that the gospel should be told through story. But the story is more than just the Christ event; it is the entire flow of the Bible narrative. So rather than extracting the gospel from the Bible, like a 'pre-packaged' proposition or an excerpt which points back to the Bible to back it up, Jesus himself *is* both the lead character and the story, throughout the Bible. The telling to Muslims of the good news about Jesus must therefore be done by seeing the whole Bible as 'the gospel'.

An example of how this works in practice can best be described by the example of Interserve – the missionary fellowship I work with – which consciously commits itself to 'wholistic mission'. This means working within the following parameters:

- the beginning (i.e. the creation purpose of God for humankind and the earth)
- the all-pervasive impact of sin (for humankind and the earth)
- the all-inclusive scope of the cross and resurrection (for humankind and the earth)
- the hope of the glorious reign of God over all.[3]

This approach is vital because the Bible does not start with the predicament of human guilt – as is common among western Christians – but rather with the creation purpose of God. Andy Matheson wrote the book *In His Image*, after spending several years bringing the gospel in word and action to the poor of South Asia. He emphasized God's love for each individual human being and his purpose for each person and the action he has taken in Christ in order to relate to each one of us as his child.[4] Matheson's crucial insight is that when we address the hearer's 'capacity' in this way, we are more able to relate to them as a human being who has dignity and one who is uniquely loved by God. This is what Mother Teresa of Calcutta was doing when she famously referred to the marginalized as 'Christ in distressing disguise'.

So when we focus on the hearer's 'deficiency' it is easy to lose sight of their intrinsic value to God. So the 'deficiency' approach is less appropriate because in Middle Eastern culture, bad news is worked around to in conversation; it is never just blurted out, as an introduction. So the fact of our inherent sinfulness and need in God's eyes belongs more naturally towards the *end* of the gospel story, rather than the beginning.

The apostle Peter modelled the 'capacity' approach twice – once to the large Jewish audience on the day of Pentecost (Acts 2) and once to a smaller Gentile audience in the home of Cornelius the Roman officer (Acts 10). Peter started the telling of the gospel story with God's Old Testament promises of his plan to act in human history (Acts 2:14–21); then he listed the supernatural credentials of Jesus (Acts 2:22–24; 10:38); he then made reference to Jesus' divinity (Acts 2:25–36; 10:42); and then his cross and resurrection (Acts 10:39, 40). This gospel presentation prompted the hearers to identify themselves as being in need (i.e. deficient) and they asked: 'What should we do?' (Acts 2:37). It was at that point that Peter said they must 'repent and be baptized . . . in the name of Jesus Christ for the forgiveness of your sins' (Acts 2:38–39; 10:43).

Having said that the whole Bible contains the gospel for Muslims, there are various ways to use it. Anything that helps a Muslim to get a sense of the chronology of the Bible is likely to be more helpful. Another way is to tell the story by referring to the following catalogue of illustrations which help to illumine some of the pearls that lie along the storyline:

1. **God is knowable**. While Muslims believe God is unknowable, the good news is that he is not only 'knowable' but he is also a 'self-revealer' who has been searching for relationship with humankind since the Garden of Eden where in Chapter 4 we saw the LORD Jesus came calling out 'Adam (i.e. mankind), where are you?' (Gen. 3:9).
2. **God is concerned about the behaviour of human beings**. For Muslims, God cannot be touched by our human situation, but the gospel says that God does have emotions, such as the day when 'the Lord

regretted that he had made human beings on the earth, and his heart was deeply troubled' (Gen. 6:6, NIV); similarly, 'God so loved the world that he gave his one and only Son' (John 3:16) who also had a deep compassion for people (Matt. 23:37–39; John 11:35).

3. **God loves human beings unconditionally**. Islam teaches that God's love is conditional and reserved only for those who love him. The gospel says that God not only responds with love to those who love him, but that he loves everyone (Jer. 31:3; John 3:16; Rom. 5:6–8), and even that God is love (1 John 4:16).

4. **God's character is consistent.** Islam does not expect God to be consistent, because this would compromise his sovereignty; his unrestricted power means he can change (or 'abrogate') his word as he pleases. As a result, Islam has a problem reconciling God's mercy and his justice. The gospel says that God is indeed consistent, so there are certain things he 'cannot' do, such as act against his character, so his word cannot be changed because it springs from his character, not his whim. Also, at the cross, the requirements of mercy and justice were perfectly met. I find that 'penal substitution' seems unjust to Muslims, but it can help to explain that the gospel is not just that 'Christ died *for* us' (i.e. instead of us) but also that 'we died *in* Christ' (i.e. his death transferred our 'shame' and 'guilt' to himself). We died *with* him.[5]

5. **God is a triune unity**. The gospel says that the Trinity represents a totally unified rescue team where 'God the Father' planned it, 'God the Son' enacted it, and 'God the Spirit' implements it.

6. **Jesus is included in the divine name**. While Islam teaches that Jesus was just a prophet who was only a

'created being' (S.3.59), the gospel says that Jesus is eternal, which sets him apart from all others – including Muhammad.

7. **Jesus marks the fulfilling of the law**. Islam insists on compliance with religious law (*shari'a*), but Jesus brought a new way of relating to God (Ezek. 36:25–28; Jer. 31:33) freeing us from religious law and placing us under a new law – the 'law of the Spirit of life' (Rom. 8:2).

8. **Jesus has authority over the spirit realm today**. Jesus is able to defeat the activity of the devil and the harassment of demons (*jinn*), which operate in the lives of some Muslims (Matt. 10:1; Luke 9:1; 10:19; 1 John 3:8).

Jesus' life, death and resurrection carries special significance for people in shame-orientated societies, as demonstrated by his repeated healing of people deemed to be 'defiled' or 'ritually unclean'. The gospel writers structured their material about him in such a way as to highlight his honourable credentials. Matthew made repeated references to his public prestige and social standing: 'his fame spread all over Syria' (Matt. 4:24–25, RSV); 'Herod the tetrarch heard about the fame of Jesus' (Matt. 14:1, RSV); and his 'honour' was shown by the fact that great crowds followed him (Matt. 13:2; 14:13; 15:30; 19:2; 21:9–11; 22:33).[6]

The Kingdom of God and the Muslim

The gospel story can be told through Jesus' teaching about the kingdom of God, particularly in his Sermon on the Mount (Matt. 5:1 – 7:29). Jesus' words speak to the heart-hunger of Muslim people rather than their mental prejudice. I am indebted to Gerard Kelly for his insight into Jesus' Sermon on the Mount and the skill with which he captures the implications – in contemporary language – for the western mind. By doing this, Kelly identifies the way in which Jesus' words challenge both the 'eastern' concept of 'honour' and also its western counterpart of 'power'; both of which confront one another today as East and West try to foster political, economic and theological forms of supremacy over one another.

> Popular western culture insists that to be first is to be best and only those who excel are able to become icons of our age. All who do not attain this stage of excellence and domination are considered inadequate. It is here that the gospel kicks in and insists that inadequacy is the truth about us all.[7]

The Sermon on the Mount challenges the value systems which drive all cultures, reversing the definition of what it means to be truly 'honourable' in God's sight. For example, one picture we gain from Jesus about the power of the kingdom of God is the ability/willingness of Jesus' followers to 'resist, absorb and transform' the same aggressive selfish interests which pervade western liberal democracies as much as some Islamic states.

Right use of the law

The Sermon resonates with enquiring Muslims because in it, Jesus was returning the theme of religious law back to its rightful function as a tutor, 'put in charge to lead us to Christ' (Gal. 3:24, NIV). The Mosaic law was like an ethical scaffold that supported the values of the kingdom of God, while the Spirit of God worked in them.

Kelly goes on to show that although we can embrace the grace of God in an instant, it takes a lifetime for its effects to percolate our fallen human nature to the point where the scaffold of religious law becomes redundant and can be dismantled.

Absorbing evil by non-violence

The Sermon on the Mount also challenges many Muslims – and a worrying number of Christians – for whom the 'eye for an eye' principle of the *torah* is preferable (see Exod. 21:34; Lev. 24:20; Deut. 19:21) to the 'turn the other cheek' principle of the Kingdom (Matt. 5:39). Jesus was not abolishing the *torah* when he taught us to absorb evil; on the contrary he was fulfilling it by highlighting the spirit behind it (Matt. 5:17). The 'eye for an eye' system provided a mechanism for 'restorative justice'. This provided fair recompense for a wrong that had been suffered by an individual, while drawing a line under the misdemeanour and avoiding an escalation of violence through 'tit-for-tat' acts of revenge that can go on for years.

Jesus raised the standard set by the law of Moses, in that while the *torah* permitted 'eye for eye, tooth for tooth, hand for hand' (Exod. 21:24), he went on to say: 'do not [even] resist an evil person. If anyone slaps you on the right cheek, turn to them the other cheek also' (Matt. 5:39). The word 'resist' (*anti-stenai*) means to 'stand against'. This is a military metaphor used by the apostle Paul when he urged followers of Jesus to 'put on the full armour of God' so they could 'withstand' (*anti-stenai*) the attacks of the devil; and when they had done everything else they were to 'stand' (*stenai*; Eph. 6): a form of non-aggressive resistance. So when Jesus urged his followers to 'turn the other cheek' he was providing a more appropriate response to the backhanded slaps that were given to local people by Roman soldiers and which would catch the person on the right cheek; behaviour that was intended to degrade rather than injure. To present the face in this way prevented a further strike, but it was also a non-verbal way of asserting that you were a human being and had the right to dignity. This form of assertiveness without violence was the way to achieve what Paul taught when he said: 'Do not repay anyone evil for evil' (Rom. 12:17).

This kingdom value of passive resistance was adopted by an unusual admirer of Jesus – Mahatma Gandhi – who referred to it as *satyagraha* ('truth-force'); the practise used to lead Indians in non-violent protest against the British Raj.[8]

Externalism

Muslims will also be intrigued by Jesus' teaching on 'externalism', where the 'performer' and/or the 'observer' of a religious ritual become so preoccupied with the action itself, that they lose touch with the reality the action points to. This was the perversion of the law of Moses that was going on in Jesus' day. Jesus challenged the teachers of the law, calling them 'hypocrites', a 'brood of vipers', 'blind guides' and 'whitewashed tombs' (Matt. 23). He insisted that God wants a heart relationship with people, not external religious rituals, done purely for public show: 'Be careful not to do your acts of righteousness in front of others, to be seen by them' (Matt. 6:1). This also relates to many Muslims who strive for external 'honour' while being willing to lose their integrity to do it. The apostle Paul agreed when he said: 'The law is good if one uses it properly' (1 Tim. 1:8). I have listed elsewhere some of the elements of Judaism which Islam has borrowed.[9] These religious duties (*du'a*) are expressed through the regular performance of rituals, including the five core duties of Muslims which are known as the 'pillars' of Islam (*arkân al-islam*).[10] Jesus' teaching in the Sermon on the Mount addressed three of these Islamic duties – prayer, giving and fasting.

Praying (salât)

Muslims prefer to practise prayer communally using *raka'a* (positions), including prostration. They believe that merit is gained by performing prayer, particularly on Fridays, the Islamic holy day. When I lived in the Middle East I grew used to seeing Muslims who were so concerned about appearing to be pious that they rubbed dirt into a self-inflicted wound on the forehead in order to create a scar; this made it look as if they prayed so regularly, a welt had developed on their forehead.

Jesus challenged this sort of behaviour: 'When you pray, do not be like the hypocrites, for they love to pray . . . on the street corners [i.e. to be seen *performing* it]. When you pray, go into your room, close the door and pray to your Father, who is unseen' (Matt. 6:5–6). So prayer from the heart and in private is of more value to God than public prayer.

Giving (zakât and sadaqa)

Jesus also taught about giving: 'When you give to the needy, do not let your left hand know what your right hand is doing, so that your giving may be in secret' (Matt. 6:3–4). This phrase has passed into the English language, as has the story Jesus told about 'the widow's mite'. In this parable, a poor widow gives her last penny to God, while a wealthy man gives a relatively large amount out of his vast fortune, without even missing the money. Jesus used the story to teach that giving should be from the heart and therefore personal, sacrificial and discreet, rather than an ostentatious performance (Mark 12:42–43).

Fasting (sawm)

> The same is true about Jesus' teaching on fasting: 'When you fast, do not look sombre as the hypocrites do, for they disfigure their faces to show others they are fasting . . . But when you fast, put oil on your head and wash your face, so that it will not be obvious to others that you are fasting . . .' (Matt. 6:16–18).

Social standing

Jesus was speaking in the presence of Jewish religious professionals. To these Pharisees the people who deserved the sermon were the 'shameful' – tax collectors (i.e. collaborators with Rome) and 'sinners' (i.e. the 'lost' or *daalleen* in Arabic); such people were treated with disdain. Yet at the same time Pharisees expected people to 'honour' them, as the outwardly pious. Jesus, however, did the opposite and gave 'honour' to the 'lost', while insulting the religious elite by implying in parables such as the lost sheep that the Pharisees and teachers of the law were the failed shepherds of Israel who had let the sheep scatter (Luke 15:1–10). Jesus was identifying them as the ones who the prophets condemned for failing to tend Israel – the flock of God – and that they should accept responsibility for this (Ezek. 34). Kenneth Bailey points out that in Middle Eastern societies – particularly in Bible times – the role of keeping livestock of any sort was a ritually unclean occupation that was usually assigned to people of low social standing and/or doubtful morals.[11]

This is why Joseph's family were seen as 'detestable' by Pharaoh when they visited Egypt (Gen. 46:31–34) – a fact that adds poignancy to the nativity story, where it was shepherds who were summoned first by angels to witness the arrival of the Christ-child. This turns upside-down the categories in which Muslims understand the world.

The Kingdom is Good News for Muslims

In the kingdom of God the 'shamed' become 'honourable', the losers become the winners, the poor are the true wealthy and the rich are the true poor. It is not God who is wrong here but our fallen human race, which Dallas Willard described as 'flying upside down'.[12]

Jesus modelled the values of the Kingdom by being born into poverty, not privilege; he walked the margins of society and not the corridors of power. He set the record straight about how God has always intended things to be from creation morning onwards, but which got deviated by our rebellion against him in the Garden of Eden. Jesus placed the marginalized at the centre and banished those at the centre to the margins. True 'honour' is found by identifying ourselves with Jesus Christ in this epic story of redemption.

> Only salvation offered to losers – whether by circumstance or by choice – can be described as comprehensive. There is nothing you don't have that can bar you from entry to this kingdom – only the things you have might keep you out.[13]

Not far from the kingdom?

When a Muslim is in touch with his own need and can accept that he is unable to help himself, he is not far from the kingdom of God. The next thing is that he takes the all-important step of praying: 'God, have mercy on me, a sinner' (Luke 18:13). When this plea comes from a bankrupt heart, it releases God's grace. Oswald Chambers was clear that repentance brings, not so much a sense of sin as a sense of unworthiness. 'When I repent, I realize that I am utterly helpless. I know all through me, that I am not worthy even to bear his shoes. Have I repented like that? Or is there a lingering suggestion of standing up for myself?'[14]

More Muslims than ever are identifying with the sentiment expressed by King David when in Psalm 51 he prayed for God's grace to save him. He used the external legal language such as 'sin', 'verdict', 'guilt' and 'forgiveness', while also speaking about internal shame using words such as 'purity' by 'washing' and 'cleansing' from 'defilement' of sin. This prayer was prophetic in that it was spoken way ahead of its time, anticipating the day when Messiah would arrive and become God's grace-filled solution to the human predicament of 'sin', 'guilt', 'shame' and 'defilement' – once and for all:

Have *mercy* on me, O God, according to your unfailing love; according to your great compassion blot out my *transgressions*. *Wash* away all my iniquity and cleanse me from my sin.

For I know my transgressions, and *my sin* is always before me. Against you, you only, have I sinned and done what is evil in your sight; so you are right in your *verdict* and justified when you judge.

Surely I was *sinful* at birth, sinful from the time my mother conceived me . . . *Cleanse me* with hyssop, and I will be clean; *wash me* and I will be whiter than snow . . . Hide your face from my sins and *blot out* all my iniquity.

Create in me a *pure heart*, O God, and renew a steadfast spirit within me. Do not cast me from your presence or take your Holy Spirit from me. Restore to me the joy of your salvation and grant me a willing spirit, to sustain me.

You do not delight in sacrifice, or I would bring it; you do not take pleasure in burnt offerings. My sacrifice, O God, is a broken spirit; a broken and contrite heart you, God, will not despise. (italics mine)

This psalm describes the end of a Muslim's journey to Christ and the beginning of a life following him. It is in this secret place, that they can find the reality of the Arabic expression *'mastûr al-hâl'* – 'the shame is covered'! This is a phrase that is used as a resolution after an inter-personal conflict. It reassures both parties that they are exonerated and the matter has been put to rest.

The good news for Muslims is that at the cross, 'shame' was transferred from them to Christ and washed by blood to purify us (1 John 1:7). So God is indeed saying to a Muslim 'The shame is covered; go in peace'!

Below are some illustrations which help to show Muslims the significance of Jesus' death, which made it possible for us to be absolved from the effects of 'shame':

Symbol 1: Jesus the sacrificial lamb atoning for shame

It is good news for Muslims that Jesus covered our shame by transferring it to himself on the cross, from where he carried it away into hell. The use of the word 'cover' here is important because it is the root meaning of the word 'atone' from which we derive the word 'atonement'. Adam and Eve were 'covered' when the LORD (i.e. Jesus) apparently slaughtered an animal to provide skins with which to cover their shame (Gen. 3:21). Also in the Jewish festival of Yom Kippur, or Day of Atonement, the lifeblood of a lamb 'covered' (i.e. protected) an entire household from evil (Exod. 12). The Lord Jesus became the Passover Lamb at the cross where his blood covered our shame (1 Cor. 5:7–8).

The tragedy is that while the cross is the solution to 'shame', it has also become the stumbling-block for Muslims who are taught that it is impossible for a prophet of Islam, such as Jesus, to suffer such shame. They prefer the Islamic legend that says Judas was crucified in Jesus' place (S.4.157–8). In spite of this objection, the incarnation was the culmination of God's search for relationship with humankind; the search began in the Garden of Eden (Gen. 3:9) and ended on the cross (1 Pet. 2:24). It is clear from the numerous detailed prophecies about the crucifixion that the cross was a carefully planned event. The prophet Isaiah described the crucifixion as follows:

He was despised and rejected by others, a man of suffering, and familiar with pain. Like one from whom people hide their faces he was despised, and we held him in low esteem. Surely he took up our pain and bore our suffering, yet we considered him punished by God, stricken by him and afflicted.

But he was pierced for our transgressions, he was crushed for our iniquities; the punishment that brought us peace was on him, and by his wounds we are healed. We all, like sheep, have gone astray, each of us has turned to our own way; and the LORD has laid on him the iniquity of us all (Isa. 53:3–6).

Symbol 2: Jesus the scapegoat

On the cross, Jesus became the ultimate personification of the Old Testament 'scapegoat' (Lev. 16:10). The tabernacle priests would lay hands on the goat, confessing the sins of the people. The sin was then symbolically transferred to the goat before it was released outside the camp as an act of abandonment whereby it was ignored and nothing more done for it. The writer to the Hebrews described Jesus as fulfilling this role as he 'suffered outside the city gate to make the people holy through his own blood' (Heb. 13:12). As the ultimate 'scapegoat' who absorbed the sin, guilt and shame of the world, God the Father withdrew from Jesus, prompting him to call out: 'My God, my God, why have you forsaken me?' (Matt. 27:46). The writer to the Hebrews invites us all to 'go to [Jesus] outside the camp, bearing the disgrace he bore' (Heb. 13:13). This is an apt description of the challenge and the cost – particularly to Muslim people – of changing allegiance to follow Christ.

Symbol 3: Jesus the **Qurbani** *lamb*

About two months after Ramadan, Muslims celebrate the feast of *Eid-ul-Adha*; a feast that involves the sacrifice (*qurban*) of a lamb. This is seen as an act of self-denial rather than the biblical idea of atonement. The feast commemorates the incident in Genesis 22 where Abraham's faith was tested when he was instructed by the angel of the LORD (i.e. Jesus) to offer up his son as a human sacrifice like pagan people did for their gods. This posed a moral dilemma to Abraham, who was also in danger of losing face in the eyes of other desert chieftains.

Abraham discounted the idea that faith was a bare surrender to the will of God. He believed that it required an exercise of reasoning so that the will of God could be understood and justifiably followed. But he also believed that such enquiring faith should seek out the mind and purpose of God behind his will, and promptly proceeded to do this in respect of the command to sacrifice his son. Such is true discerning faith, and for such faith Abraham was deeply commended by God.[15]

As Abraham started to go through with the sacrifice of his son, he was stopped by an angel and a substitute ram was found nearby (Gen. 22:11–14). Many Muslims are mistakenly taught that the son referred to in the Genesis 22 account was Ishmael; however the Qur'an only mentions Isaac when it says God gave Abraham 'good news of *Isaac*' (S.37.112–13, italics mine). The sense of the text suggests that this 'good news' was that – in the words of the Qur'an – 'when (the son) reached the age of serious work [puberty], he [Abraham] said: "O my dear son! I see in a vision that I [must] offer thee in sacrifice"' (S.37.100–102). The text goes on to say: 'We *ransomed* him [i.e. the son] with a momentous sacrifice' (S.37.107, italics mine), which is not only in line with the Bible's account but also reflects the language of redemption.

An important parallel emerges here between Isaac and Jesus. Isaac carried the wood up Mount Moriah on which he was to be offered as a sacrifice. Centuries later, Jesus too carried the wood – this time a cross – on the same mount where he was sacrificed as 'the Lamb of God' for the life of the whole world (John 1:29). Abraham did not withhold 'his only son' (Gen. 22:12) and neither did God '. . . spare his own son but gave him up for us all' (Rom. 8:32).

Symbol 4: Jesus the brass serpent

The cross was enacted centuries before it happened, when a plague broke out among the Hebrews in the wilderness under Moses' leadership. The Bible says that 'the LORD' (i.e. Jesus) instructed Moses to put a brass serpent on a pole so that the people who had been bitten by serpents could look towards the brass serpent and be healed (Num. 21:8–9). Jesus later claimed to be the direct fulfilment of this incident: 'As Moses lifted up the snake in the wilderness . . . when I am lifted up from the earth, I will draw all men to myself' (John 3:14; 12:32).

The cross as successful failure

Muslims need to understand that the cross of Christ was an honourable success and not a shameful failure. The success of the cross was graphically told by C.S. Lewis in his book *The Lion the Witch and the Wardrobe*. The victory was won when Aslan voluntarily gave up his power and authority to embrace failure. This broke the curse and split the stone table. Lewis based this on Jesus, who intentionally embraced shame on our behalf so that we need never be 'ashamed' (Ps. 119:80; 2 Tim. 2:15). Far from being a failure, the cross of Christ was the final solution to the shame issue:

> See, I lay a stone in Zion, a chosen and precious cornerstone, and the one who trusts in him will never be put to shame (1 Pet. 2:6, italics mine).

> 'The blood of (Old Testament) goats and bulls . . . sprinkled on those who are ceremonially unclean sanctify them so that they are outwardly clean. How much more, then, will the blood of Christ . . . cleanse our consciences

[i.e. damaged by both guilt and shame] from acts that lead to death, so that we may serve the living God!' (Heb. 9:13–14)

'fixing our eyes on Jesus, the pioneer and perfecter of faith . . . he endured the cross, scorning its shame, and sat down at the right hand of the throne of God' (Heb. 12:2).

The gospel for Muslims says that God and suffering are perfectly compatible and even inevitable; a discovery made by theologian Jürgen Moltmann, who was born in 1926 and converted while a prisoner of war. In his classic book, *The Crucified God* he said:

A God who cannot suffer is poorer than any human, for a God who is incapable of suffering is a being who cannot be involved. Suffering and injustice do not affect him . . . so in the end he is also a loveless being. In declaring himself to be love, God is committing himself to being involved with the world he has created.[16]

C.S. Lewis pointed out that love involves pain; the greater the love, the greater the suffering involved.[17] American sociologist Willard Walker spent a lifetime studying human relationships, and concluded that in any relationship the one who loves the least has more power and the one who loves the most has least power. He called this the 'law of least love'. The cross of Christ is a vivid demonstration of the powerlessness of love.[18] 'God *is* love' (1 John 4:16, italics mine) and through his suffering on the cross, the Lord Jesus shamed 'shame', holding it up to ridicule, breaking shame's curse on us, transferring it to himself and in so doing, breaking the back of the spiritual principalities and powers of evil (Col. 2:15).

A striking example of someone whose life was blighted by 'shame' was an Indonesian Muslim woman whose husband had divorced her, leaving her destitute with a family to raise on her own. To make enough money to keep the family together, the woman was forced into prostitution. When the eldest daughter was old enough to understand what was going on, she would feel her mother's hair in the mornings. If it was damp, her mother had been with clients the night before. It was more unthinkable for the woman not to take a ritual bath after having sex, than it was to commit the act of fornication itself.[19] For each act that leads to defilement in Islam, there is an appropriate remedy to restore ritual purity. This concept is included in the *torah*, which says 'when a man has sexual relations with a woman . . . both of them must bathe with water, and they will be unclean till evening' (Lev. 15:18).

Anthropologist Mary Douglas has done important research into the culture of the Jews under *torah* and the notion of what was 'clean' or 'unclean', 'defiled' or 'hygienic'. She points out that the dietary rules of the book of Leviticus – such as the prohibition against pork – would be inconsistent with God's pronouncement that the whole of creation was 'very good' (Gen. 1:31).[20] So to suggest that pork was inherently 'unclean' is misleading, and we need to look elsewhere for the reason for such prohibitions – for example, the fact that there was a health issue in preserving pork safely in a hot climate. Having said this, Douglas also found a relationship between the concept of 'contagion' and moral values because 'defilement' had the useful social function of marshalling moral disapproval should ritual cleanliness lapse and prescribed rituals were then used to restore order.

So to be 'ritually clean' can be as serious an issue in the eastern mind as exoneration in the law courts might be to the western mind. For Muslims, it is not so much a matter of getting rid of the sense of 'guilt' for wrongdoing as avoiding 'defilement' that causes 'shame'. The subconscious question for many Muslim people is therefore more likely to be: 'Can I be moved from a position of shame to a position of honour – and if so, how?'

The gospel for Muslims has been expressed well by Christian leaders in shame-orientated societies. They describe how God drove out defilement from the human condition by becoming flesh. Jesus' life, death and resurrection were all linked together to become one honourable action. Eastern Christians look at the cross and see Jesus driving out darkness like a candle entering a dark room. For them, Jesus' death and passion moved us:

- from illegitimacy to being a child of God
- from being far from God to being near him
- from falling short to being complete in Christ
- from being blind to seeing
- from accusation to exoneration
- from self-defence to being represented before God
- from life under curse to being blessed
- from spiritual poverty to having riches in God.[21]

Muslim-background believers in Jesus in South Asia define their experience by using the relational and participatory expression 'in Christ' (Rom. 6:1–8) to describe how they were with Christ in his death and resurrection and ascension – rather like a letter in an envelope that is *en route* to a destination.

We have seen that the idea of 'penal substitution' is unjust in the minds of Muslims but the 'in Christ' language of eastern believers in Jesus couches the truth in an eastern way. It is not just that 'Christ died *for* us' but also that 'we died *in* Christ'. These Asian believers also see the cross as an act of grafting them into the fellowship of the triune *elohim* in the same way that a sapling vine is grafted into a healthy branch (John 15:1–8; see also Rom. 11:11–24). The system of grafting is still used in Middle Eastern agriculture today where they make a cross-shaped incision in the branch and insert the new sapling before binding it up to let it bond. When the process is complete the two become one unified organism and it is difficult to tell where the sapling ends and the branch starts. For 'eastern' followers of Jesus, the emphasis seems to be more on where we are in Christ – i.e. *now* – and less on how we got there; of course, both aspects must be held in tension.

I hope enough has been said to establish that there is hope for the 1.3 billion Muslim people alive in the world today; and it is my prayer that this book inspires you to believe that Muslims you know can turn to Christ. To care about the eternal destiny of a Muslim will automatically give you the right attitude towards them and the desire to help them understand how the gospel that began in the East, applies directly to them. And so we come to the end of a book that is a love-gift to all Muslims and Christians who read it. By writing it, I am identifying myself with other like-minded people – many of them visionaries and apostles of love from around the world and down the years – who have impacted my life. These are people who, like me and my friend Irfan, are dreaming the impossible dream that I believe comes from the heart of God, who calls into being 'things that were not' (Rom. 4:17).

The recent political convulsions in the Arabized world appear to be the birth pangs, which may help to deliver the 'reformation' that Islam has never had. We can therefore engage ordinary Muslims in the knowledge and humility that, ultimately, we will see the redemption of the house of Islam. In that day multiplied millions more Muslims will yet 'call on the name of the LORD and be saved' before he returns (Joel 2:31–32).

Notes

[1] Wright, Tom, *Justification: God's Plan and Paul's Vision* (London: SPCK, 2009), p. 221.

[2] Wright, Tom, *Justification: God's Plan and Paul's Vision* (London: SPCK, 2009), p. 222.

[3] *God's Big Idea: Wholistic Mission* (Kuala Lumpur: Interserve International Vision & Practice Series, 2010), p. 4.

[4] Matheson, Andy, *In His Image* (Milton Keynes: Authentic Media, 2010).

[5] I am grateful to Tim Green for this insight used in his leader's guide to the course, *Friendship First: Ordinary Christians Discussing Good News with Ordinary Muslims* (Milton Keynes: Interserve Resources, 2011).

[6] Neyrey, Jerome, H., *Honor and Shame in the Gospel of Matthew* (Louisville: Westminster John Knox Press, 1998), p. 36.

[7] Kelly, Gerard, *The Jesus Driven Life – a Rough Guide to the Sermon on the Mount* (Milton Keynes: Authentic, 2001), p. 25.

[8] Stott, John, R.W., *Christian Counter-culture* (Leicester: IVP, 1978), p. 109.

[9] Bell, Steve, *Grace for Muslims – the Journey from Fear to Faith* (Milton Keynes: Authentic Media, 2006), pp. 69–74.

[10] Bell, Steve, *Grace for Muslims – the Journey from Fear to Faith* (Milton Keynes: Authentic Media, 2006), pp. 65–7.

[11] Bailey, Kenneth E., *Jesus Through Middle Eastern Eyes – Cultural Studies in the Gospels* (London: SPCK, 2008).

[12] Willard, Dallas, *The Divine Conspiracy – Rediscovering Our Hidden Life in God* (London: Fount, 1998), p. 7.

[13] Kelly, Gerard, *The Jesus Driven Life – a Rough Guide to the Sermon on the Mount* (Milton Keynes: Authentic, 2001), p. 8.

[14] Chambers, Oswald, *My Utmost for His Highest* – 22 August, Revised Edition, ed. J. Reimann (Grand Rapids: Discovery House Publishers, 1992).

[15] Gilchrist, John, *The Christian View of the Eid Sacrifice*, Christianity and Islam Series No. 6 (South Africa: FFM, 1979), p. 22.

[16] Moltmann, Jürgen, *The Crucified God: The Cross of Christ As the Foundation and Criticism of Christian Theology* (London: SCM Press, 1973).

[17] Lewis, C.S., *Mere Christianity* (London: Penguin, 1959).

[18] Chalke, Steve, and Mann, Alan, *The Lost Message of Jesus* (Grand Rapids: Zondervan, 2000), pp. 182–3.

[19] Bruce, Thomas, 'The Gospel for Shame Cultures: a Paradigm Shift'. *Evangelical Mission Quarterly*, 1994.

[20] Douglas, Mary, *Purity and Danger: an Analysis of the Concepts of Pollution* (London: Ark Paperbacks, 1966).

[21] Muller, Roland, *Honour and Shame: Unlocking the Door* (New Jersey: Xlibris Corporation, 2000).

Interlude

Azerbaijani Muslim woman finds Jesus in Britain

I grew up in Azerbaijan where most people are liberal Muslims. This is because they were educated under an atheistic regime when Azerbaijan was part of the Soviet Union. Although I believed in one God, Allah, it was impossible for me to imagine the possibility of having relationship with him, let alone my having any assurance of going to heaven.

When I was 22 years old I was diagnosed with leukaemia. This forced me to deal with the reality of death for the first time. After a traumatic two years of medical treatment, God did an amazing thing and miraculously healed me.

When I left Azerbaijan to move to Britain in order to study for a Masters degree, I didn't know that it would be there that I would personally encounter Jesus Christ in my life. This all began when I started to attend church services and some Christian events for international students in my university in the north of England.

I became desperate to know who Jesus was. I wanted to get to the bottom of the claim that he had died for me, so that I could live with him for ever. It was about six years ago that I gave my life to Jesus Christ. Since then God has been doing amazing things in my life through his Holy Spirit; changing my heart every day and enabling me to be a witness to his grace.

I know that God has always had plans for me because he saved me physically and then spiritually.

I have been living in Asia for the last three years where I have been seconded by Interserve as a professional volunteer with a local Christian organization. I am thankful to God for this wonderful opportunity to serve him.

My new motto in life is: 'To show his love, Jesus died for me; to show my love, I will live for him.'

Newcastle, 2009

Appendix A:

Jesus in the Old Testament

Chapter 4 outlined several of Jesus' appearances throughout the Old Testament. The accounts below equally suggest that the mysterious visitor could not logically have been anyone else other than Jesus, as well as demonstrating his divinity as a member of *elohim*.

Visits to Jacob

Abraham's grandson Jacob was also granted audiences with the LORD. He reported that 'God Almighty' (i.e. *el-shaddai*) 'appeared' to him at Luz where he also 'blessed' him and 'spoke' to him (Gen. 48:3–4). The visitations to Jacob started in Genesis 28 when he was sent off to his extended family in Harran to find a bride; a practice continued today by many Muslim families. En route to his family, Jacob created an overnight makeshift bed in the desert where he had a dream of what is referred to as 'Jacob's Ladder'; this was a 'stairway' ascending from the desert floor into heaven, with angels going up and down on it. At the top of the stairway 'stood' the LORD (Gen. 28:13) which indicates again that he had the form of a man. The LORD identified himself to Jacob as 'the

God of your father Abraham'. He entered into conversation with Jacob and spoke with divine authority about Jacob's future, the land which he would inherit and about his future life under the protection of the divine name of *elohim* (Gen. 28:13b–15).

Jacob spent fourteen years working for his uncle Laban to procure the hand of his cousin Rachel as a wife (Gen. 29). While he was finally travelling back to Canaan, Jacob had his most dramatic encounter with the LORD who approached again in the form of 'a man', with whom Jacob wrestled through the night until dawn (Gen. 32). True to his distrusting nature, Jacob asked the LORD for his name. This was more than a casual request for some personal identification; it was an eastern enquiry to gain the knowledge which was a means of penetrating the visitor's identity. In eastern cultures, people keep something back and do not reveal everything because a name is a gateway to the core of their being, in the same way that a personal password makes our personal information accessible on a computer. In some societies people literally have a secret name for this reason. The LORD refused to divulge his name to Jacob, but 'blessed him' instead. The notion of a hidden name is reflected in the book of Revelation (Rev. 2:17b; 3:12–13) when the LORD'S true identity will at last be made known to the entire cosmos, which will worship him.

Like his grandfather Abraham before him, Jacob's blessing also included a name change; this time from 'Jacob' to 'Israel' (i.e. one who 'struggles with God'). This marked the fact that Jacob had 'struggled with God . . . and overcome' (Gen. 32:28). The text goes on to say that Jacob called the place of encounter 'Peniel' (i.e. face of God), saying, 'I saw God face to face, and yet my life was spared' (Gen. 32:30). Like Hagar before him, Jacob met the LORD and knew that he was in the presence of *elohim*.

After arriving back in Canaan, the LORD appeared to Jacob for the last time, to bless him and reaffirm the promise that was symbolized by the name change (Gen. 35:9–10). On his deathbed, Jacob invoked this promised blessing of the divine name of *elohim* to come upon his son Joseph and his two grandsons, Ephraim and Manasseh. In doing this, Jacob referred to the LORD as 'the God before whom . . . Abraham and Isaac walked . . . the Angel who has delivered me from all harm' (Gen. 48:15–16). In all these appearances, the LORD was identified as divine.

The Appearance in the Book of Joshua

In Joshua 5 – 6, the LORD came to meet Joshua in the guise of the 'Commander of the Lord's Army' (Josh. 5:14). In the New Testament Jesus is referred to in a similar way as 'head over every power and authority' (Col. 2:10). Joshua saw 'a man' with a drawn sword who did not seem to be an angel *per se* but a warrior. This is something akin to his appearance in the book of Revelation where he is revealed in all his glory to lead out the army of God in the final assault against the forces of evil (Rev. 19:11–16). This is the sort of 'power' imagery that resonates well with the Islamic respect for strength and ability to influence. Muslims need to be aware that this is also a facet of Jesus.

The Appearances in the Book of Kings and the Prophets

At the start of his reign, King Solomon was visited by the LORD in a dream where he was invited to ask whatever he wanted in order to enhance his reign (1 Kgs. 3:5). Solomon famously chose wisdom not wealth, so the LORD made him the most opulent of all the kings of Israel.

When Solomon had completed the building of the temple in Jerusalem, the LORD appeared to him again to confirm that he had accepted the consecrating of the temple and that his eyes and his heart would always be there. This was a poignant point in view of his forth-coming relationship with the temple in the Gospels. The LORD also warned Solomon to be careful to follow him as his father David had done (1 Kgs. 9:5–14). Sadly, by the end of his life, the LORD was angry with Solomon because although he had appeared to him twice, he did not end his reign well (1 Kgs. 11:9).

King Ahaziah was injured by falling through his con-servatory roof. He sent a delegation to enquire of a local deity whether he would recover (2 Kgs. 1). This promp-ted the angel of the LORD to instruct the prophet Elijah to intercept the delegation and challenge them that such information was only obtainable from himself – the God of Israel. He sent the message to Ahaziah, via Elijah, that the king would not recover. The king ordered Elijah's arrest which Elijah resisted by calling down fire from heaven on two groups of soldiers who attempted to bring him in. The captain of a third consignment fell at Elijah's feet and begged that their lives would be spared. The angel of the LORD intervened again to reassure Elijah that it was alright to go with the men. Elijah went with them and delivered the bad news of non-recovery to King Ahaziah in person. The king later died, according to the word of the LORD.

The Appearances in the Psalms

Psalm 2 gives a fascinating insight into the relationship between God the Father and his 'anointed' (i.e. Messiah or Christ) (v. 2b). The role and function of the 'anointed one' is identical to that of 'the angel of the LORD' i.e. included in *the divine name* (v. 3). In this psalm 'the LORD God' gave his anointed position (v. 6); the anointed spoke as the word of 'the LORD God' (v. 7a); God the Father conferred on the LORD the title 'Son of God', which means that he was inseparably connected to him like a genetic family. He was also the heir of all things pertaining to God the Father (v. 7b), who decreed that the only way to find refuge from his wrath was in his Christ, who becomes like a rock of refuge (v. 12b).

Psalm 110 extols the virtues of the LORD who is the ultimate warrior, monarch and priest. The psalm is not about David but 'David's Lord' (i.e. the LORD Jesus). God speaks to Jesus and says, 'Sit at my right hand until I make your enemies a footstool for your feet' (v. 1). David's 'Lord' is also identified as being at the divine 'right hand' and the one who will judge the world.

The Appearance in the Prophecy of Isaiah

Isaiah feared for his life when he saw the LORD. He said 'my eyes have *seen* the King, the LORD Almighty' (Isa. 6:5). The LORD was in the form of a man who was 'seated on a throne' and surrounded by seraphim which were above him; the train of his robe 'filled the temple' (v. 1). All these phrases describe a figure that looked like a man, but was in fact God. Isaiah did not die as he expected, but received a prophetic commission instead.

The Appearance to the Prophet Ezekiel

Ezekiel encountered *elohim* when he approached the prophet with the familiar seismic disturbances we associate with his presence – 'windstorm', 'cloud', 'lightning', 'brilliant light' and 'fire' (Ezek. 1:4). Ezekiel saw the same throne that the prophet Isaiah had seen in the past (Ezek. 1:26; Isa. 6:1); this was also what the apostle John would see later in the book of Revelation (Rev. 4:2).

Ezekiel heard 'the voice of one speaking' (Ezek. 1:28): a characteristic of 'God the Word' (see Rev. 1:12; 19:13). The prophet then saw 'the form of a man' who appeared to be clothed with fire (Ezek. 1:26–28): the same thing the apostle John saw on Patmos, when he described Jesus' appearance as being like 'bronze glowing in a furnace', 'blazing fire' and 'the sun shining in all its brilliance' (Rev. 1:13–16). Both Ezekiel and John fell face down in his presence (Ezek. 1:28b; Rev. 1:17).

This was the scene that Ezekiel described as 'the likeness of the glory of the LORD' (Ezek. 1:28b). He encountered *elohim* as God Almighty (i.e. the Father) who came near in all his majesty (Ezek. 1:4–24). At the same time God the Word (i.e. Jesus) commissioned him (Ezek. 1:3, 25a, 28b; 2:1) and as God the Spirit came into him and lifted him up (Ezek. 2:2; 3:12, 14).

Appendix B:

Fulfilled prophecy about Jesus Christ

1. Jesus would be born in Bethlehem (Mic. 5:2; Matt. 2:1)
2. Jesus would emerge from Galilee, which is where Nazareth is (Isa. 9:1; Matt. 4:15)
3. Jesus would have a virgin birth (Isa. 7:14a; Matt. 1:23a)
4. Jesus' arrival on earth would constitute 'God with us'(Isa. 7:14b; Matt. 1:23b)
5. Jesus would be identified as the 'Son of God' (Ps. 2:7; Matt. 3:17)
6. Jesus' arrival would be greeted by dignitaries (Isa. 60:3; Matt. 2:1–12)
7. An attempt would be made on Jesus' young life (Jer. 31:15; Matt. 2:16–18)
8. Jesus would be taken to Egypt (Hos. 11:1; Matt. 2:13–15)
9. Jesus would be heralded by a forerunner (Isa. 40:3–5; Matt. 3:1–3)
10. Jesus would be meek and gentle (Isa. 42:2–3; Matt. 11:29)
11. Jesus would gravitate to the vulnerable (Isa. 40:11; Matt. 11:28–30)

12. Jesus would be a miracle worker (Isa. 35:5–6; Matt. 4:23)
13. Jesus would be praised by children (Ps. 8:2; Matt. 21:15–16)
14. Jesus would enter Jerusalem in triumph (Zech. 9:9; Matt. 21:1–11)
15. Jesus would clear the temple (Ps. 69:9a; Matt. 21:13)
16. Jesus would be betrayed by a friend (Ps. 41:9; Matt. 26:14–16)
17. Jesus would be abandoned by his followers (Zech. 13:7; Matt. 26:31, 56b)
18. Jesus would be bought for thirty pieces of silver (Zech. 11:12–13; Matt. 26:15)
19. Jesus would be accused by false witnesses (Ps. 35:11–12; Matt. 26:59–61)
20. Jesus would be derided by his enemies (Ps. 22:7–8; Matt. 27:38–44)
21. Jesus would be rejected by men (Isa. 53:3; Matt. 27:15–26)
22. Jesus would be scourged and spat on (Isa. 50:6; Matt. 27:26; 26:67)
23. Jesus' body would be pierced (Ps. 22:16; Zech. 12:10; John 19:37; 20:26–27)
24. Lots would be cast for Jesus' clothes (Ps. 22:18; Matt. 27:35)
25. Jesus would be led like a silent lamb to his death (Isa. 53:7; Matt. 27:12–14)
26. Jesus would be given vinegar to drink (Ps. 69:21; Matt. 27:34; John 19:28–29)
27. Jesus would cry out in anguish when forsaken by God (Ps. 22:1; Matt. 27:46)
28. Jesus would pray for his persecutors (Isa. 53:12c; Luke 23:34a)
29. Jesus would be buried in a rich man's tomb (Isa. 53:9; see also Matt. 27:57–60)

30. Jesus would be raised from death (Ps. 16:9–11; Matt. 28:7)
31. Jesus would ascend to heaven (Ps. 24:7–10; Acts 1:9–11)
32. Judas' place among the apostles would be taken by another (Ps. 109:8; Acts 1:15–26)

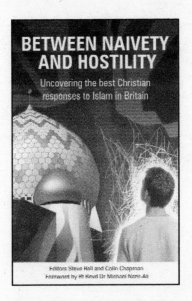

Between Naivety and Hostility

Uncovering the Best Christian Responses to Islam in Britain

*Editors Steve Bell
and
Colin Chapman*

Every day news stories appear around the world about Muslims and Islam. In the UK the tabloids often express the fears and anxieties of many people about the growing numbers and influence of Muslims in Britain. But should there be anything distinctive about the way Christians respond to these issues? While some demonize Muslims and Islam, others do not see anything to be concerned about. Is there a middle way between these two extremes – a response that avoids both naivety and hostility?

In this book, twenty committed Christians give some helpful answers. They are all actively engaged with Muslims and aware of the realities on the ground. They all stress the need to build genuine relationships of trust and respect with Muslims.

978-1-85078-957-4

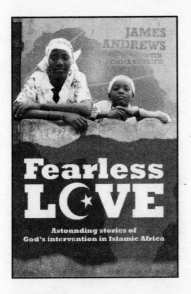

Fearless Love

Astounding Stories of God's Intervention in Islamic Africa

*James Andrews
with
Emma Newrick*

The Bible college you can read about in *Fearless Love* is based in a city in northern Nigeria, in the vicinity of the huge Islamic 'harvest field' of the African Sahel, just south of the Sahara desert. Until recent years the city had seen less killing of Christians than regions nearby. The founding team believed it would be a safe hub in which to train those God calls from the surrounding regions and nations to spread the gospel far and wide. However, as this city is a centre of gospel outreach the Islamic community is also aware of its strategic importance . . .

Fearless Love is a deeply challenging and informative book that tells the story of the college's mission to reach people with the gospel in the midst of Islamic jihad – in a hostile region where being a Christian, and especially converting to Christianity, may easily cost you your life.

978-1-85078-982-6

Grace for Muslims?

The Journey from Fear to Faith

Steve Bell

'Why should an essentially "benign" religion turn some into "demons"?' asked a Muslim journalist. It is a question that is at the heart of the Islamic debate. Alarmist claims are made about these 'demons', while the possibility of a peaceful Islam is dismissed. Many are confused about the religion's contradictory faces.

Is it possible for Christians to relate to Muslims without being politically naïve or theologically liberal? Steve believes it is. He shares his own journey and reflects upon how he arrived at the crucial ingredient – grace.

978-1-85078-664-1

Son of Hamas

A Gripping Account of Terror, Betrayal, Political Intrigue, and Unthinkable Choices

Mosab Hassan Yousef

Son of Hamas is now available with an all-new chapter about events since the book's release such as the revelation of Mosab's Israeli intelligence handler's true identity, and Homeland Security's effort to deport the author. Since he was a small boy, Mosab Hassan Yousef has had an inside view of the deadly terrorist group Hamas. The oldest son of Sheikh Hassan Yousef, a founding member of Hamas and its most popular leader, young Mosab assisted his father for years in his political activities while being groomed to assume his legacy, politics, status . . . and power. But everything changed when Mosab turned away from terror and violence, and embraced instead the teachings of another famous Middle East leader. In *Son of Hamas*, Mosab reveals new information about the world's most dangerous terrorist organization and unveils the truth about his own role, his agonizing separation from family and homeland, the dangerous decision to make his newfound faith public, and his belief that the Christian mandate to love your enemies is the only way to peace in the Middle East.

978-1-85078-985-7

Authentic

We trust you enjoyed reading this book from
Authentic Media Limited. If you want to be informed
of any new titles from this author and other exciting
releases you can sign up to the Authentic Book
Club online:

www.authenticmedia.co.uk/bookclub

Contact us
By Post: Authentic Media Limited
52 Presley Way
Crownhill
Milton Keynes
MK8 0ES

E-mail: info@authenticmedia.co.uk

Follow us: